DAVID WILLIAMSON's first full-length play, *The Coming of Stork*, premiered at the La Mama Theatre, Carlton, in 1970 and later became the film *Stork*, directed by Tim Burstall.

The Removalists and *Don's Party* followed in 1971, then *Jugglers Three* (1972), *What If You Died Tomorrow?* (1973), *The Department* (1975), *A Handful of Friends* (1976), *The Club* (1977) and *Travelling North* (1979). In 1972 *The Removalists* won the Australian Writers' Guild AWGIE Award for best stage play and the best script in any medium and the Britain production saw Williamson nominated the most promising playwright by the London *Evening Standard*.

His success continued in the 1980s with *Celluloid Heroes* (1980), *The Perfectionist* (1982), *Sons of Cain* (1985), *Emerald City* (1987) and *Top Silk* (1989); the 1990s produced *Siren* (1990), *Money and Friends* (1991), *Brilliant Lies* (1993), *Sanctuary* (1994), *Dead White Males* (1995), *Heretic* (1996), *Third World Blues* (an adaptation of *Jugglers Three*) and *After the Ball* (both in 1997), *Corporate Vibes* and *Face to Face* (both in 1999). *The Great Man* premiered in 2000.

Williamson is widely recognised as Australia's most successful playwright and over the last three decades his plays have been performed throughout Australia and produced in Britain, United States, Canada and many European countries. A number of his stage works have been adapted for the screen, including *The Removalists, Don's Party, The Club, Travelling North, Emerald City, Sanctuary* and *Brilliant Lies*.

David Williamson has won the Australian Film Institute film script award for *Petersen* (1974), *Don's Party* (1976), *Gallipoli* (1981) and *Travelling North* (1987) and has won eleven Australian Writers' Guild AWGIE Awards. He lives on Queensland's Sunshine Coast with his wife, writer Kristin Williamson.

ALSO BY DAVID WILLIAMSON FROM CURRENCY

Brilliant Lies
The Club
Corporate Vibes / Face to Face
Dead White Males
The Department
Don's Party
Emerald City
The Great Man / Sanctuary
Money and Friends
The Perfectionist
The Removalists
Siren
Sons of Cain
Top Silk
Travelling North

COLLECTED PLAYS VOLUME I: *The Coming of Stork*; *The Removalists*; *Don's Party*; *Jugglers Three*; and *What If You Died Tomorrow?*

COLLECTED PLAYS VOLUME II: *A Handful of Friends*; *The Club*; *The Department*; and *Travelling North*.

ABOUT DAVID WILLIAMSON

Brian Kiernan, *David Williamson: A Writer's Career*
This authoritative account of Williamson's phenomenal career draws on his early writings, unpublished drafts, letters and journal entries; as well as the recollections of friends and colleagues.

STUDY GUIDES for *The Club* and other Williamson plays are available from the Currency website:

www.currency.com.au

THE CLUB
(*Players*)
DAVID WILLIAMSON

CURRENCY PRESS · SYDNEY

Currency Plays
General Editor: Katharine Brisbane

First published in 1978 by
Currency Press Pty Ltd
PO Box 2287
Strawberry Hills NSW 2012
www.currency.com.au
enquiries@currency.com.au

Reprinted in 1979 (twice), 1981, 1982 (twice), 1983, 1984, 1986, 1989 (twice), 1992, 1993, 1994, 1995, 1996, 1997, 1998, 1999, 2000.

Copyright © David Williamson, 1978

Copying for Educational Purposes:
The Australian *Copyright Act* 1968 allows a maximum of one chapter or 10% of this book, whichever is the greater, to be copied by any educational institution for its educational purposes provided that the educational institution (or the body that administers it) has given a remuneration notice to Copyright Agency Limited (CAL) under the Act. For details of the CAL licence for educational institutions please contact CAL, 19/157 Liverpool Street, Sydney, NSW 2000, tel (02) 9394 7600, fax (02) 9394 7601, email: info@copyright.com.au.

Copying for Other Purposes:
Except as permitted under the Act, for example a fair dealing for the purposes of study, research, criticism or review, no part of this book may be reproduced, stored in a retrieval system, or transmitted in any form or by any means without prior written permission. All inquiries should be made to the publisher at the above address.

Any performance or public reading of *The Club* is forbidden unless a licence has been received from the author or the author's agent. The purchase of this book in no way gives the purchaser the right to perform the play in public, whether by means of a staged production or a reading. All applications for public performance should be made to the author, c/o Curtis Brown, PO Box 19, Paddington, NSW 2021.

NATIONAL LIBRARY OF AUSTRALIA
Card number and ISBN 0 86819 013 6

Typeset by Queensland Type Service Pty Ltd
Printed by Star Printery Erskineville, NSW

CONTENTS

The Greatest Game of All, Lou Richards   vii
Winners and Losers, Ian Turner   x
THE CLUB   1
The Play in the Theatre, Rodney Fisher   74

Ron Barassi (Carlton) in action. Photo by courtesy of *The Age*.

THE GREATEST GAME OF ALL
Lou Richards

David Williamson must have pinched half his lines for *The Club* from a fly on a committee room wall. His mastery of ocker footy lingo is so word perfect you'd swear he was given Ron Barassi's old athletic support for his first birthday and had board and lodging at Jack Dyer's place.

There is more sting in some of the lines here than in all the backstabbing at a social club bar on a Saturday night.

As you will see when you read on, he has put it all together beautifully and come up with a cutting play about the real business of the modern Aussie Rules back-room boys—dirty business. It is a simple plot about a once-successful footy club that hasn't won a premiership in nineteen years. Run by a wheeler-dealer, meat-pie manufacturing megalomaniac of a president who has never pulled on a boot and who interferes with the selection committee, the Club is having trouble with its expensive, imported star; trying to get rid of its loyal, long-time coach and facing a strike from the rest of the team.

David Williamson may not see it—he says he is writing a play about organisational power—but if you can't recognise among the people you know the characters and situations in *The Club*, then you've either spent the last few years in a Tibetan monastery or you're a New South Welshman. In fact, that's why it's such a pleasure to write this introduction. Footy and its followers have been my life. I spent many of the happiest years of my life playing for Collingwood and with Collingwood people. I must admit I've never known a footballer who became a lover to his mother and his 'legless sister', as Jock so subtly puts it; but each of Williamson's six characters is spot-on. It won't take much to recognise the guys who run your club, no matter what team you follow.

Take Gerry, the ruthless, new-breed career administrator. Every club has at least one—the sort of guy who makes the bullets for all the other bunnies to fire. And there are plenty of footy *führers* like the blustering president, Ted—frustrated footballers who have followed their side every Saturday arvo since they were six. They might mean well, as Ted does, but they carry on like petty little dictators, sticking their noses where they ain't wanted. And what about Geoff, the fabulous, flashy import, who doesn't give a continental about the Club and its proud traditions or the photos of past greats hanging on the walls? Can't you just see him in a fancy pair of white footy boots?

Probably the truest part in the play, though, is that of Laurie— the poor old coach who, as is customary it seems when a team is down, finds his head the first one for the chopping block. And talk about nostalgia. Tears come to my eyes when I think of Danny, the skipper and long-time club champion who is about the get the axe after years of selfless service. It's just like it was 1955 all over again and I'm about to get the old heave-ho as captain of my beloved Maggies. But best of all I like Jock, the conniving, interfering ex-president, former champion and jealous holder of the Club's longest player record. When I saw the play he was played impeccably by my old mate Frank Wilson. It was a perfect character—a sure thing for an award from the Sacked Coaches Association. So there it is. I felt like I knew each of the six. I'm sure you do too—that's half the fun of the play. *The Club* is about the hangers-on, the end of loyalty, the coming of professionalism, big business and massive transfer fees. It's about each and every club in the Victorian Football League and about rugby, soccer and baseball too.

But for me it's mainly about Aussie Rules football—the greatest game in the world. Good move, David Williamson!

Gary Dempsey (Footscray) breaks clear with the ball in a match against Hawthorn. Photo by courtesy of *The Age*.

WINNERS AND LOSERS
Ian Turner

What is *The Club* about? I suppose you could say that it's about Melbourne—because Melbourne is about football, and the club is a football club. Melbourne, someone once said, is a city that has no summer; instead, it has a hibernation between football seasons. Every Saturday afternoon, from April to September, more of the people of Melbourne (a city of some two and a half millions) go to the football than attend the soccer in any one week in the United Kingdom. (Note that 'football' in Melbourne means Australian Rules—soccer and rugby and gridiron are something else again.)

You can, if you want to—and many do—watch or listen to football previews on television and radio on Thursday and Friday night and Saturday morning; go to the game on Saturday afternoon, listening while you watch to the broadcast reports of other games; and come home to replays and inquests on Saturday night, Sunday, and Monday evening. (The daily and weekly newspapers fill in the gaps left by the electronic media.)

An amateur sociologist once calculated that the opening gambit—after the conventional exchange of "How do you do?" or, "Hi"—in 83·5 per cent of Melbourne conversations was 'Which team do you follow?' In Melbourne, team-identification is more important than religion, profession or social class. Football is Melbourne's Saturday afternoon corrida: dying fans have asked that their bodies be buried between the goal-posts or their ashes scattered over the hallowed ground.

So in one sense *The Club* is about Melbourne, an otherwise dour and inward-turning city, which has this one grand public passion. For all I know, it may be about Liverpool and Milan and Notre Dame as well. 'The game of the people for the people' is the official motto of Melbourne football. The clubs exist to serve the football followers—that's the theory. *The Club* explores the quality of the service, and the motives of those who supply it.

Modern football is part of the popular entertainment industry. It has its performers, its managers, its promoters and plenty of hype. There isn't as much money in the game (at least in

Australia) as there is in, say, pop music or the movies. But the rewards—money, fame, prestige, power and the fringe benefits which go with them—are big enough to make them worth fighting for. Football is about all those things, but there is more to it than that. It is also about loyalty to people, to an institution and a tradition, and about pride in craftsmanship. And, like all games, it is about winning and losing. British (and Australian) 'sportsmanship' is not an ethic of indifference to the result of the game; it is a code of conduct which regulates the competition. Melbourne football coaches demand of their players that they 'contest fiercely'; there is a tribunal to ensure that they contest within the rules.

The entertainment industry has its own internal contradictions—if we wanted to be pretentious, we could call them structural polarities. Suppliers and consumers do not necessarily agree about what constitutes good entertainment; hype reinforces rather than creates the response. Buying and selling performers, in an endeavour to maximise the chance of winning, cuts across established patterns of identification and loyalty. Managers and promoters have their own idea of what constitutes success, and their own axes to grind; they often tramp heavy-footed over the professional pride of the performers whom they seek to manipulate. *The Club* is about those contradictions; with the necessary changes in detail, it could probably be taken out of the club's committee room and dropped into the back rooms of Hollywood, Wardour Street or Tin Pan Alley.

Football is, in formal terms, a game—a rule-governed contest. But the players/performers are not 'playing'; the game is far too serious for that. Football is no fun for the big league footballers. For them, it may be about social mobility and financial gain, and whatever kicks a charismatic hero gets out of dominating his audience. But there is almost always in it, for the players, the craftsman's satisfaction in a job well done. *The Club* is about that too.

So *The Club* is a play for many seasons—but above all a play for one season: Melbourne, in the long winter months.

'Tiger-territory'
Melbourne, 1977

John Newman (Geelong) makes a spectacular leap over Terry Alexander (Collingwood). Photo by courtesy of *The Age*.

THE CLUB

Above: Gerard Maguire as Gerry, Frank Wilson as Jock and Frank Gallacher as Ted in the Melbourne Theatre Company production, 1977. Below: Frank Gallacher with Terence Donovan as Laurie. Photo: David Parker.

Above: Terence Donovan as Laurie and John Walton as Geoff in the Melbourne Theatre Company production. Below: the full cast—Gerard Maguire, Frank Wilson, Harold Hopkins as Danny, Terence Donovan, Frank Gallacher and John Walton. Photo: David Parker.

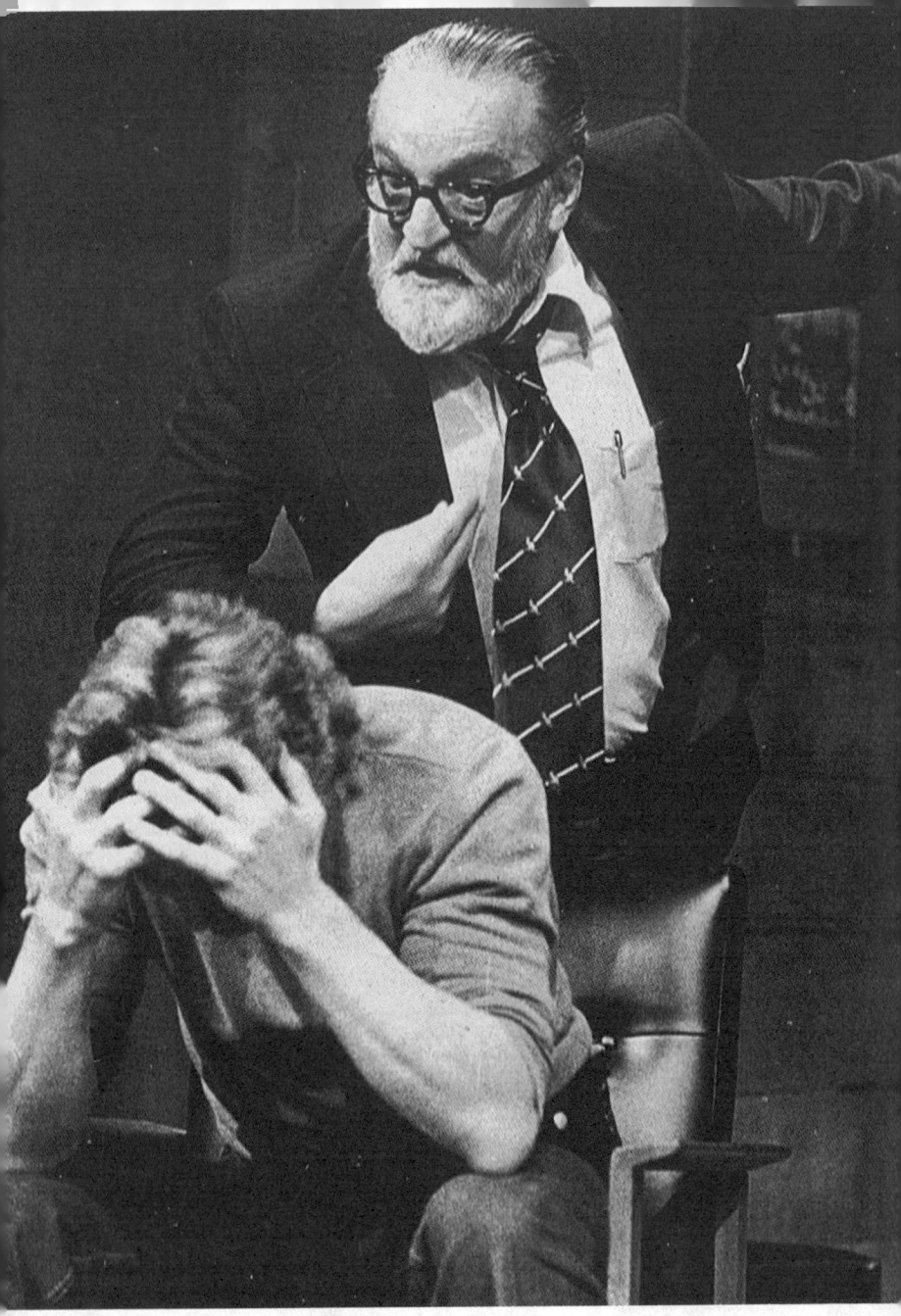
John Walton and Frank Wilson. Photo: David Parker.

The Club was first performed by the Melbourne Theatre Company at the Russell Street Theatre, Melbourne, on 24th May 1977 with the following cast:

GERRY	Gerard Maguire
TED	Frank Gallacher
LAURIE	Terence Donovan
DANNY	Harold Hopkins
JOCK	Frank Wilson
GEOFF	John Walton

Setting designed by Shaun Gurton
Directed by Rodney Fisher

CHARACTERS:

GERRY COOPER
TED PARKER
LAURIE HOLDEN
DANNY ROWE
JOCK RILEY
GEOFF HAYWARD

SETTING:

The action of the play takes place in the committee room of a top professional football club. A formal committee table surrounded by chairs is seen towards the back of the stage. Lounge chairs and a coffee table dominate the downstage area. It is in this area that most of the action takes place. Large, framed head-shots of former club champions adorn the walls. A door on the left leads to the general and recreational areas of the club building, while to the right a door leads to a private bar used by committee members.

ACT ONE

GERRY COOPER, *lean, alert, in his middle thirties, sits on the table smoking, a folder in one hand.* TED PARKER *enters from left. He is small, pudgy, manic, nervous, in his early forties.*

TED: Good.
GERRY: Good what?
TED: Good that you're early.
GERRY: Always early.
TED: Going to be tough.
GERRY: What?
TED: *(more clearly)* Going to be tough.
GERRY: Who? Laurie?
TED: No. The whole business. Going to be awkward. It'll have to be handled carefully. My first impulse is to blast hell out of him. Really blast hell out of him. He's hurt me, Gerry, and I'm angry. Really angry, but I think it's much better if I stay cool. Don't you think so? Better to stay cool?
GERRY: If you stay as cool as you are now we're all in trouble. Calm down.
TED: Sometimes it takes more courage to hand out the olive branch than to jump in boots and all. I'm not going to smile and pretend that it didn't happen mind you, but I'm going to stay cool.
GERRY: Calm down.
TED: I could use a drink.
GERRY: ~~Grab a bottle of Scotch from next door.~~ Grab one.

(TED *nods and goes out, right.*)

TED: *(off)* How's June?
GERRY: Sick.
TED: *(off)* That's great. Sick?
GERRY: Mmm.

TED *re-enters with a bottle of Scotch and two glasses.*)

TED: What's she got?
GERRY: 'Flu.

[margin note: scene needs a lot more energy]

TED: There's going to be a new 'flu strain in the next ten years that's going to wipe out nine tenths of the world population.
GERRY: Yeah?
TED: I read it in the Sunday papers.
GERRY: That'll test Medibank.

(TED *pours them each a whisky. The left door opens and* LAURIE HOLDEN *comes in.* LAURIE *is a tall well-built man in his middle forties. There is an awkward silence.* TED *inclines the whisky bottle towards* LAURIE. LAURIE *declines*.)

TED: I'm sorry it's come to this, Laurie.
LAURIE: So am I.

(*There is another awkward pause.*) [handwritten: more awkward]

June better yet, Gerry?
GERRY: Improving, thanks, Laurie.
LAURIE: Give her my love.
GERRY: Will do.
TED: Thanks for coming, Laurie. The Committee thought it might be better if we tried to thrash this out privately before tonight's meeting.
LAURIE: Fine.
TED: The Committee wants to see if you and I can settle our differences, Laurie. They don't want to accept your resignation.
GERRY: I thought I'd come along to see if I can act as an impartial sounding board for you both. Jock was going to come along and lend a hand too, but as usual he's late.
LAURIE: Jock? Lend a hand?
GERRY: His idea, not ours, but once he gets an idea in his head he's a little hard to discourage. We'll go if you two get to a point when you'd rather talk things through yourselves.
TED: The Committee's unanimously of the opinion that they don't want to lose you, Laurie. You're one of the

best coaches we've ever had and you've given the Club great service.

GERRY: We'd find it very hard to replace you, Laurie.

(*There is another pause.*)

TED: The Club's going through a slump but nobody blames you.

LAURIE: I should bloody well hope not.

TED: (*exploding*) Holy Jesus, Laurie. There's no need to be totally self righteous. When a football club performs as badly as ours has over the last five weeks, most coaches would be honest enough not to try and absolve themselves of *all* the blame. ~~It really makes me wonder whether there's any point to this exercise when I come to you in a spirit of conciliation and you jump down my throat at the first opportunity.~~ I was hurt by what you said about me in the press, deeply hurt. It took all my self control to be pleasant to you when you walked in that door.

GERRY: I think I should tell you that the Committee took a pretty dim view of your press statements, Laurie. If you had any grievances you should have come to us.

LAURIE: The press asked me if it was true I was handing in my resignation, so I said yes, and they asked me why, so I told them.

GERRY: How did they know about your resignation before we did?

LAURIE: I don't know.

GERRY: Did you tell the players you were about to resign?

LAURIE: Yes. I felt I owed it to them.

TED: You must have known they'd take it to the press.

LAURIE: I thought it was a possibility. I didn't ask them to.

GERRY: It puts the Committee in a hell of a position when you criticise the Club President in the press, Laurie.

TED: What's my sin, Laurie? ~~What's my crime?~~ All I could get out of the article was some vague accusation that I was autocratic. What exactly were you trying to say? That I have opinions? All right. I'm guilty. ~~That on occasions I express them? All right. Guilty again~~. Just what am I expected to do, might I ask? Go away and hide in a corner? I'm the Club President, Laurie. I was elected by the members to lead this Club and I'll bloody well lead it, and if anybody tries to stop me I'll crush them. No, Gerry. I'm sick of pussyfooting around. I'm going to speak my mind. He's called me autocratic so he just better come up with some evidence.

LAURIE: I wouldn't know where to begin.

(There is a knock at the door and DANNY ROWE enters. He is twenty-eight, small and nuggetty.)

TED: What do you want?

DANNY: I want to know what's happening.

LAURIE: It's all right, Danny. I can handle it.

DANNY: *(to GERRY)* The players want their point of view heard before the committee makes any decision about Laurie.

TED: The players can go to hell.

DANNY: They always could as far as you were concerned, Parker, but we'd just like the Committee to know that we're a hundred percent behind Laurie.

TED: Well, you can just go and tell the players that the Committee are a hundred percent behind me.

DANNY: Then perhaps the Committee had better roll up and play tomorrow's match.

TED: What's that supposed to mean?

DANNY: It means that if that bloody Committee of yours gives Laurie the boot tonight, then we don't play tomorrow.

LAURIE: Come off it . . . *(Danny)*.

TED: This is lovely. Really delightful. A strike threat.

LAURIE: ~~Danny.~~ Go home and calm down.

TED: A strike threat.

DANNY: It's no threat. We mean it. You sack Laurie tonight and you won't have a team tomorrow.

TED: Sack him? ~~What do you mean sack him?~~ He's

bloody well resigned. We're not sacking anyone. Did you hear that, Gerry? A strike threat? (*To* DANNY) You won't find me bending under that sort of pressure, my boy.

LAURIE: There'll be no strike whether I'm here or not.

TED: I should bloody well hope not. ~~There's more than enough industrial anarchy in the community at large without us copping it on the football field. Next thing you know they'll be holding a stopwork meeting every time the umpire blows his whistle louder than fifty decibels.~~

DANNY: Very funny. You'll be sneering on the other side of your face tomorrow.

GERRY: Danny, if you'd just clear off we'll get this whole thing sorted out.

TED: Laurie offered his resignation and we're treating it seriously. What else do you expect us to do?

DANNY: He only offered to resign because you bloody well drove him to it. How could any coach run a team with you sticking your nose in everywhere?

TED: Sticking my nose in?

LAURIE: I appreciate this, Danny, but you're doing me more harm than good. Go home and calm down.

DANNY: Someone's got to tell him.

TED: What do you mean sticking my nose in?

DANNY: It's not your job to pick the bloody team.

TED: I don't. I'm not even on the Selection Committee.

DANNY: No, but you take two thirds of 'em up to the bar and talk for four hours every Wednesday night.

TED: Jock and Tony? So what? The team is barely discussed.

DANNY: That's not what I heard.

TED: Then you'd better rap your spies over the knuckles because the team is barely discussed. Laurie, have you ever thought I've tried to influence the selection of the team?

LAURIE: Yes.

TED: When?

LAURIE: This week.

TED: That's a lie.

LAURIE: You told Jock and Tony that Geoff Hayward wasn't to be dropped.

TED: I didn't *tell* them any such thing. I expressed an opinion that he shouldn't be dropped and they happened to agree with me. ~~Aren't I allowed to express an opinion? Am I supposed to go around this place with adhesive tape over my mouth.~~ I might have known that Geoff Hayward was at the bottom of all this. ~~What have you all got against him?~~ He's struggling for form at the moment but he's an absolute champion. What have you got against him?

LAURIE: Nothing. He's playing badly and should be dropped to the reserves.

TED: That's your opinion, but the other two selectors happen to agree with me. Tough luck. Don't try and make a conspiracy out of that. In my opinion it's no wonder the lad's a bit out of touch. The team's made him feel as welcome as a blowfly at a butcher's picnic.

DANNY: I'm sorry. We were all going to give him a big kiss, but we thought he'd be in a hurry to get home and count his money.

TED: We're not still back on that issue, surely? The Club did not pay a hundred thousand for him as reported in the press—

DANNY: I know. You paid eighty.

TED: How did you know?

LAURIE: I told him.

TED: Thanks. That was meant to be confidential. Geoff didn't get it all. His club got the bulk of it. My God, if what you're trying to tell me is that the team's playing badly because it's still sulking over a little bit of money that went into the pocket of a legitimate champion then I'm disgusted.

DANNY: There are a lot of legitimate champions in this club, Parker, and all we got for joining was a guernsey and a pat on the back. ~~I've given the Club ten years of my life and all I've got in the bank is eighty dollars.~~

TED: Well you must be a hell of a fast spender, Rowe.

You're on a bloody good contract and you're due for your provident fund when you retire.
DANNY: I can hardly wait. I'm taking my two best friends out to a Pizza Palace and putting the other half in the bank.
TED: You've done pretty well out of the Club, Rowe. If you can't organise your finances then that's your fault.
DANNY: What's that meant to mean, Parker?
TED: Nothing more than what I said.
GERRY: This is all beside the point. We've spent the money on Hayward and there's nothing much we can do about it. If you don't think he's worth his place in the team you're entitled to want him dropped, Laurie, but if Jock and Tony vote against you it's scarcely a reason to go running to the press.
LAURIE: The press came to me. I didn't go to them.
GERRY: All right, but you didn't have to talk to them. Could we steer this discussion back to more fruitful areas? Danny. I think we've got the players' point of view now, thank you.
DANNY: We want to know the outcome.
GERRY: All right. Wait outside.

(DANNY *moves reluctantly to the left door and goes outside, closing it after him.*)

Right, well it seems we've got a bit closer to the real seat of the problem. You think Ted's been interfering in team selection and more specifically that he's been protecting Geoff Hayward?
LAURIE: No, it's not just that. I resent the fact that he's come into the Club with no background and no experience and carried on as if he's God almighty.
TED: I was elected by the members of this Club on a platform of reform and I intend carrying it through.
GERRY: In what other ways has Ted interfered, Laurie?
TED: I haven't interfered in any bloody way!
GERRY: I'm just trying to get at the facts, Ted.
TED: I know what he resents. He resents the fact that I've brought a level-headed business approach to the

Club, and that that approach is going to bear fruit. That's what he resents. He'd like to take us back to the days of the glorious Club tradition.

LAURIE: Rubbish.

TED: We might have the proudest tradition in the League but we haven't won a premiership in nineteen years. Tradition, tradition, tradition. We've been strangled by it. ~~The days when recruits would flock to the Club from all over the country simply because of its name are long since gone.~~ It's no good waiting for players to come to you; you've got to go out there into the marketplace and fight for them.

LAURIE: I've been asking the Committee to buy players for years and you know it. Don't give me a lecture on tradition.

TED: All right. So why are we fighting? I've gone in there and battled with the bloody diehards and for the first time in the Club's history we're buying players.

LAURIE: You're buying the wrong bloody ones. I could have bought *three* players for the money you spent on Hayward, and every one of them would've been more use to the team than he is.

GERRY: (*looking at his watch*) We're getting nowhere. Could I have a word to Laurie alone, Ted?

TED: Sure. I want this thing sorted out as much as you do, Laurie. I'll go and get some cigarettes.

(*He goes to the door on the left, opens it, and turns to them.*)

Where's all that spirit we had when I was elected last year. It can't have evaporated. Remember my election slogan? The great leap forward—boom or bust. What happened?

DANNY: (*off*) We bust.

TED: (*turning to him, heatedly*) We came seventh and if we had've had Geoff Hayward in the team we would've made the finals. You've all been against Geoff from the minute he came here, but his first two games this year were brilliant, Laurie. You can't deny that. Absolutely brilliant.

LAURIE: And his last five have been ratshit.
TED: Give him a chance, Laurie, and give me a chance too.

(*He leaves through the left door, glaring at the unseen* DANNY.)

GERRY: (*tersely*) What the hell did you go to the press for?
LAURIE: I got fed up. I've had enough of that clown.
GERRY: I've been at my wit's end trying to contact you. Tony said he found you at home.
LAURIE: I was.
GERRY: I've been phoning you all day. Didn't you hear it ring?
LAURIE: Yeah. I sat there listening to it while Helen made me cups of tea. It was the most relaxing day I've had in years.
GERRY: Well it wasn't for me, cobber. Not at all. You're the type who give administrators nightmares. You bottle up your grievances for months and don't say a word and suddenly I pick up my morning newspaper and bang, it's all there on page one.
LAURIE: I've had enough, Gerry. That little cretin's been trying to tell me how to do my job ever since he was elected. I'm a professional and I shouldn't have to put up with it. Not from the owner of a meat pie factory who's never played a game of football in his life.
GERRY: He was elected by the members and so were four of his cronies. They've got the numbers and we're stuck with them.
LAURIE: He's got to go and that's final.
GERRY: You're scarcely in a position to be delivering ultimatums, Laurie. The Committee are on the point of accepting your resignation.
LAURIE: Then they'd better accept it. I can't go on this way. Geoff Hayward turned up three quarters of an hour late for training last night, I told him to do twenty push-ups and he told me to get stuffed. Three hours later, courtesy of Ted Parker, he's picked in the team.

GERRY: Ted's not on the Selection Committee and you are. Did you tell Jock and Tony that Geoff had defied you?

LAURIE: No, but I told them I wanted him dropped. That should've been enough.

GERRY: They're not just your puppets, Laurie. They've got minds of their own. Why didn't you tell them that the lad had defied you?

LAURIE: Because it isn't easy to admit that you can't control one of your players. It shouldn't have been necessary in any case. He's been playing atrociously. Did you see last week's game?

GERRY: Yes.

LAURIE: He ignored all my instructions, wandered down to the forward line, and stood there staring out into the crowd. And when the ball came downfield he just stood there watching it go past. I'm not exaggerating, Gerry. He stood there and watched it go past.

GERRY: Yes, I did see that incident. What's wrong with him?

LAURIE: I don't know, but it might help if he didn't feel that he had the unconditional support of the Club President.

GERRY: Yeah, well Ted does feel pretty committed to him.

LAURIE: He was the one who authorised us spending all that money on him.

GERRY: It goes a bit deeper than that. Keep this absolutely confidential, but Ted kicked in with an extra ten thousand out of his own pocket.

LAURIE: He must have money to burn.

GERRY: He hasn't now. His firm's about to go bankrupt.

LAURIE: Don't expect me to cry. He came down from the grandstand last week and tried to tell me how to run the game.

GERRY: Really? That's a bit much.

LAURIE: He's never played a game of football in his life.

GERRY: He is a problem.

LAURIE: I thought the stuff I said in the press might

have embarrassed him into resigning.
GERRY: Embarrass? You couldn't embarrass Ted Parker. I lost my temper the other day and told him he was a cunning little rodent and he took it as a compliment. I wish you had've come to me instead of going to the press, because none of this need have happened. He's going to have to resign soon in any case.
LAURIE: Ted?
GERRY: Mmm. There's a storm coming up and I doubt whether he'll weather it.
LAURIE: What's he done?
GERRY: Got himself into real trouble. It's dynamite. I can't tell you anything else and I won't, but I can pretty well guarantee that he won't be around in a month or two, and you'll just have to take my word for it.
LAURIE: This is not some kind of trick?
GERRY: It's no trick. I want him out as much as you do, so patch it up, withdraw your resignation, and in a month's time or even less, he'll be gone.
LAURIE: This puts a different light on things.
GERRY: I want the clown out as much as you do.
LAURIE: What in the hell's he done?
GERRY: I can't say, Laurie, and that's final, but take my word, he'll be gone in a month. Withdraw your resignation.
LAURIE: I won't apologise. Verbally or in print. I meant what I said about him.
GERRY: Yeah, well he's pretty agitated at the moment, but let me have five minutes with him and I'm sure he'll be reasonable. We'll get a joint press statement out from the two of you saying that you've patched up your differences and you've withdrawn your resignation.

(GERRY *goes towards the door, looking at his watch.*)

The meeting's starting in an hour and a half. Just give me five minutes with him.

(GERRY *opens the door and indicates to* TED *that he should come in.* LAURIE *goes out of the door after* TED *comes in. They look at each other as they pass but don't speak.*)

TED: You know what I've been thinking? We should stop bending over backwards to placate him and accept his bloody resignation.

GERRY: It's a tempting thought.

TED: Why don't we?

GERRY: It's difficult to replace a coach halfway through a season, Ted, and he knows it.

TED: We're not going to renew his contract at the end of the year. Let's get rid of the bastard now.

GERRY: We're going to *try* and not renew his contract at the end of the year. He's very popular with the supporters and the players and the Committee knows it.

TED: To hell with the players and the supporters. The Committee's where the power is and we've got the numbers. Last Saturday's game clinched it. Blind Freddy could have seen that Danny was being beaten pointless, but Laurie refused to shift him until the last quarter. It lost us the game. Ian and Kevin were disgusted. They said that tradition can go to hell, that they're right with us and that Laurie is definitely getting the axe.

GERRY: I know, I had a long talk with them after the game; but they can change their minds again.

TED: They won't change their minds. Laurie is a dead duck.

GERRY: I never count anything as certain until it happens.

TED: Look, the supporters will be ecstatic when they find out who we're getting to replace him, and the players only like Laurie because he pampers them like babies. As far as he's concerned they can't do a thing wrong. Second from the bottom and five straight losses and the only explanation he can give us is that they're a bit upset, poor darlings, because Geoff Hayward got a little bit of money. It's just not good enough. They need a tough bloody hand and they're going to get it. Laurie is a dead duck.

GERRY: That blunder last week *was* pretty obvious.
TED: Blind Freddy could have seen it.
GERRY: They say he was a great player.
TED: Yes and my aunt makes great scones, but it doesn't mean she should run a cake factory.
GERRY: We can't sack him in the middle of the season.
TED: Well if he stays, he's going to have to apologise. In the press.
GERRY: He won't. Be reasonable.
TED: Why shouldn't he? He's held me up to ridicule. I'm the President, Gerry. He can apologise or resign.
GERRY: *(irritated)* Be reasonable, Ted. It's going to be nasty enough at the end of the year when we don't renew his contract. He hasn't exactly been a failure here. We've only been out of the finals once in eight years and we've been runner up twice.
TED: What's the good of being runner up? We want the premiership.
GERRY: And we'll get it, but don't make things difficult right now. Let's just issue a press statement to the effect that you've patched things up.
TED: That's not good enough. He's got to apologise.
GERRY: *(irritated)* Well he won't, so let's just be sensible.

(*The right door opens and* JOCK RILEY *enters. He's a large big boned man in his late sixties, shrewd and tough, with a battered yet expressive face.*)

JOCK: Sorry I'm late. (*Indicating the bottle*) Ah. Scotch.
GERRY: Get yourself a glass.

JOCK: Thrashed it out yet?
GERRY: Almost.
JOCK: Bad business. Where's Laurie?

(*He pours himself a stiff drink.*)

GERRY: Outside.
TED: Danny's there too.
JOCK: Danny? What's he doing here?
TED: He just popped in to tell us that if we sack Laurie

the players'll go on strike.

JOCK: (*amazed*) Strike? When?

TED: Tomorrow. They've threatened to refuse to take the field.

GERRY: Come on, Ted. They're not serious.

TED: I thought they were.

JOCK: Strike? I'll give the bastards strike!

GERRY: It's not a serious threat. Don't bring it up again.

JOCK: Strike, eh?

(JOCK *moves across to the right door and opens it.*)

Danny!

(DANNY *enters, followed by* LAURIE.)

DANNY: What?

JOCK: What's this bloody business about a strike? Did you threaten this Club with a strike?

DANNY: I told—(*Gerry that if*)

JOCK: I've never heard anything like it in my life. Who's involved? Give me their names. You're not indispensable, Rowe. No one's going to hold this Club to ransom. I'll suspend the lot of you. Who else is involved?

DANNY: The whole team. Except Geoff Hayward. It'll give him a chance to show what a real champion he is.

JOCK: This is a disgusting and despicable threat, Danny. I never thought I'd live to see the day. I played two hundred and eighty-two games for this Club and every time I ran onto the ground I felt as honoured to be out there wearing the Club colours as I did the first time.

GERRY: Calm down. We're just on the point of getting this all resolved, Jock.

TED: The Club won't tolerate threats, Rowe.

JOCK: By God it won't. If you're looking for a scrap, Rowe, you won't find me shirking the issue. What role have you been taking in this, Laurie? Have you been stirring the lads?

DANNY: No he hasn't.

LAURIE: They'll be out on the field tomorrow no matter what happens tonight.

JOCK: My God, I never thought I'd live to see the day when I'd hear the word 'strike' uttered in this room. Look at those pictures on the wall, Danny. Cheeta Ryan, the greatest centreman of all time, Warren Oates, only five foot seven but with a heart as big as a pumpkin. Mike Lenehan, Terry Dunstan, Sandy Forbes. Great names from a great club and you've got the honour of the tradition they created resting right there in your hands.

DANNY: Yes, and the shit from the present administration right up our nostrils.

JOCK: Don't get too cocky, Rowe. You're not indispensable.

TED: Just remember that any player found guilty of a gross misdemeanour can lose every cent of his provident fund.

DANNY: Bullshit.

TED: That's true, isn't it, Gerry?

GERRY: No. Look can we—(*get back to the*)

JOCK: Do you know what I want to do? I want to turn all those photographs around so they don't have to look down on this shameful scene. How would Harry Payne feel if he knew that the word 'strike' was being bandied around in this hallowed room. Just tell me that. How would he feel? The man who kicked three superhuman goals in the dying minutes of the '23 grand final and won us the flag. He'd think it'd all been for nothing. I wouldn't be surprised if he's turning in his grave right now.

DANNY: He isn't even dead.

JOCK: Harry? I went to his funeral last year.

GERRY: That was Harry Treloar.

JOCK: Shit yeah. There's so many of 'em dropping off I get confused, but it doesn't alter my argument. Dead or alive, what's happened here today is an insult to their memories. Those fellas up there on that wall are worth ten of your modern bloody player. All we hear from today's lot is whinges. About the administration, about money, about every bloody thing. In my day the

~~greatest honour a man could ever have was to pull a purple and gold guernsey over his head.~~ Those men up there didn't think about money. They got two and six a match during the Depression and would have played for nothing.

DANNY: Jesus, Jock.

JOCK: Well maybe not two and six, but not very much more and they would have played for nothing.

DANNY: Well they were stupid. If I'm out there risking a fractured skull or a ruptured spleen for the amusement of a pack of overweight drunks in the grandstand bar then I want to get paid for it.

TED: That's what you think of—

JOCK: Overweight drunks?

TED: That's what you think of your supporters, eh? The lifeblood of the Club. Overweight drunks? Let me tell you something, Rowe. Watching the game every week up there in the grandstand is more financial and business expertise than you're ever likely to meet in your lifetime. Last week I had Sir Richard Tanner on one side of me and Arthur Mowbray on the other, and for your information they were both drinking tomato juice.

DANNY: If you'd been there since morning it's probably all that was left.

TED: That's a pretty low sort of crack, Rowe. I've never been drunk to the point of social embarrassment in my life.

DANNY: Not much you—

GERRY: Come on, fellas. This is getting—(*us nowhere*)

TED: When have you ever seen me drunk, Rowe?

DANNY: The fund raising dinner for a start.

TED: I was sober all the evening.

GERRY: Fellas, this is—(*really quite beside the point*)

DANNY: You couldn't get out to that stripper fast enough.

TED: She asked me to take off her garter.

DANNY: She didn't ask you to fall flat on your face after you'd done it.

TED: You're very smart, aren't you, Rowe? Very, very smart. You just might need my signature on a clearance form one day soon. Just remember that.

DANNY: Why would I want a clearance?

TED: Because some interstate club might offer you money.

DANNY: I wouldn't take it. I'm staying here.

TED: What if you can't hold your place in the team?

LAURIE: Ignore him.

DANNY: Hold my place? What are you talking about? I'm fitter now than I ever was.

TED: You're nearly twenty-nine, Rowe, and you're slowing down and we can keep you here as long as we like, playing out the rest of your football in the reserves. Remember that.

LAURIE: Any more of this and I'm leaving.

TED: Well damn him. He comes barging in here un-invited, threatening strikes and calling me a drunk. It's about time someone brought him to his senses. He only got twelve kicks last week. I saw the statistics.

LAURIE: The number of kicks means nothing, it's the— (*way he*)

DANNY: It's the first time I've dropped under twenty since the start of the season, Parker.

TED: It's the first time you've found yourself playing against a classy opponent.

GERRY: (*irritated*) For God's sake. None of this is relevant.

LAURIE: The number of kicks means nothing. It's the way he disposes of them that counts.

DANNY: He wouldn't have taken his eyes off his grog for long enough to see what I *did* with 'em.

TED: I watched the match from start to finish and Wilson was beating you pointless whether Laurie realised it or not. You should have been shifted off him after the first ten minutes.

LAURIE: I'll deal with strategy, Parker.

TED: The team hasn't got any to deal with.

GERRY: Stop it, will you? All of you.

DANNY: (*upset, angry*) Everyone gets beaten once in a while, Parker. Wilson's a hell of a good footballer.

TED: Just remember what I said, Rowe. When you decide to go interstate and make some money you'll need our signature.

(DANNY *looks ready to smash* TED. LAURIE *calms him.*)

JOCK: Don't stretch a point, Ted.

TED: They threaten us. Why can't we threaten them?

DANNY: (*flaring*) Wilson's one of the best players to take the field since the war, Parker. It's easy for you and your business mates to sit up there and pour shit on me from behind the glass in your air-conditioned bar. Wilson would've beaten anyone in the country on the day. He was firing. No one could've stopped him.

LAURIE: You played a good game, Danny. Don't let him needle you.

DANNY: I've got twenty-five kicks a match for ten years. Game in, game out, and the first time I have a bad day he's onto me. What right have you got to sit in judgement on me, you fat turd? Get back to your pie factory.

JOCK: That's enough, Danny. Come on. You've given the Club great service and only a fool'd deny it.

TED: It's all right for him to call me a drunk, but I'm not allowed to tell him he played a bad game.

LAURIE: Shut up, Ted, or I'll thump you.

GERRY: For Christ's sake could we make a start on the real business of the evening? The Committee's meeting in under an hour and a half and we've got to have this whole thing resolved. Danny. Could you wait outside? You've left us in no doubt about the players' position. It will be taken into account.

DANNY: I'm not leaving until I hear something definite. The players want to be notified.

GERRY: All right. Play some pool downstairs. As soon as anything happens I'll let you know.

(DANNY *moves to the left door, but just as he opens it he turns to fire a last salvo.*)

DANNY: You watch the way you talk to me in future, Parker, or you'll end up getting flattened.

(DANNY *leaves*.)

TED: That's lovely. A player threatens the Club President with physical violence and nobody says a word.

JOCK: Ah shut up! You're lucky he *didn't* flatten you. You've got to be bloody tactful when a player's getting on in years, Ted. It's a hell of a shock to the system when a player you could have matched when you were younger turns round and takes you apart. I got angry about the strike stuff too, but you've got to be tactful about things like that. Tubby Robbins took me apart in the '39 Grand Final and when I got home Rosemary said, "I think you met your match today," and I thumped her one. She apologised later but by that time the damage was done.

GERRY: Has Danny's domestic life smoothed out yet, Laurie?

LAURIE: He's back with Raylene, but I don't know if it'll last. I hope it does. He's very fond of his kids.

JOCK: Raylene's a hell of a nice girl but the word is she's not a great one for hiding the sausage.

GERRY: Jock. Ted and Laurie are prepared—(*to work out*)

JOCK: Domestic strife's ruined many a great footballer. Donny Joseph's wife went off with a real estate agent the night before the '47 semi-final and he only got three kicks. What's happened to that Avis girl Danny shacked up with?

LAURIE: I wouldn't know.

TED: He's probably still paying the rent on her flat. ~~No wonder he's only got eighty dollars in the bank.~~

GERRY: Jock. Ted and Laurie are prepared to work out a joint press statement to the effect that they feel they can work together and that Laurie is withdrawing his resignation.

JOCK: Good.

TED: I expect the statement to say a little bit more than

that we can still work together.

GERRY: Well, that's for you two to work out. We all know that there are still some unresolved problems. Geoff Hayward being the most immediate.

JOCK: What's the problem with Geoff?

GERRY: He's giving us a bit of trouble.

JOCK: What sort of trouble?

GERRY: His attitude leaves a lot to be desired.

JOCK: Has he been getting uppity?

GERRY: Yes.

JOCK: He's got no reason to be. He hasn't been playing all that well. What's he been doing?

GERRY: Turning up late for training and disobeying Laurie's instructions.

JOCK: Has he now? (*To* LAURIE) Is that why you wanted to drop him? Too embarrassed to tell us you couldn't handle him?

LAURIE: I can handle him.

JOCK: Well, if he's being a young smart-arse he'll just have to cool his heels in the reserves for a few weeks. You should have told me he was playing up, Laurie. I would have gone along with you.

GERRY: Laurie thought that you and Tony and Ted had some sort of permanent conspiracy not to drop him.

JOCK: Christ, no. If he's been playing up we'll put him down like a shot.

GERRY: There you are, Laurie. You couldn't get much plainer than that.

TED: In all fairness I think I should point out that there's another side to all this. There's no excuse for Geoff turning up late to training, but it's a bit degrading for a footballer of his calibre to be asked to do twenty push-ups in front of the whole team.

JOCK: Rot. When I coached this team they did twenty push-ups and if they asked why they did another twenty. Jesus Christ, do you mean to tell me we've got to have a whole drama in the press before I get to find out that Geoff Hayward's playing up? You could have told me, Laurie. It's no sin to have one of your men play up on you. You ought to have known that. I had to lay you out behind the lockers in your first year before I got any sense out of you.

LAURIE: Those sort of methods don't work any more.

JOCK: Nonsense. A good thump never hurt anyone. Let's get the lad in here and thrash this thing out.

GERRY: We don't have to solve everything now.

JOCK: Strike while the iron's hot. I've been very worried about the lad's form recently and I'd like to get him in here and have a bit of a yarn.

LAURIE: I can handle him myself thanks, Jock.

JOCK: Maybe something's worrying him. Have you talked to him lately?

TED: Yeah, he told him to do twenty push-ups.

JOCK: Shut up, Ted. I used to talk to my boys and it always used to pay off. Remember Lofty Bluett? He was the worst tempered man I've ever seen when he first came to the Club. He talked back to me, wouldn't do what he was told on the field or off—a real nightmare. One day I sat down with him and looked him in the eye—you had to sit him down to look him in the eye—and I said, "Righto Lofty, what's worrying you, son?" and he just broke down and cried. True. Lofty Bluett cried. Nobody had ever talked to him like that before. Turned out the problem was really simple. He hadn't got a good night's sleep since he was sixteen 'cause his legs were too long for the bed. We bought him a king-sized bed and he won the Club best and fairest the very next year. Maybe Geoff just needs something simple like that.

LAURIE: Yeah. A king-sized pillow for his swelled head.

TED: It's no use, Jock. He's got it in for the boy.

JOCK: You'll talk to him if I get him in, won't you, Laurie? I feel a bit responsible for all this because I was on the sub-committee that decided to get him. Will you have a talk to him and try and thrash it out?

LAURIE: I don't see what good it will do.

JOCK: Now don't be stubborn.

GERRY: We don't have to have him in tonight.
JOCK: Strike while the iron's hot. I'll call him.

(JOCK *leaves through the left door.*)

GERRY: When Jock gets his mind set on something, there's no stopping him. I'll just go next door while you two draft your press statement. Give me a call when it's finished.

(GERRY *leaves through the right door.*)

TED: You should be a bit more tolerant of young Geoff, Laurie. He's going to be a great asset to us sooner or later.
LAURIE: Can we leave Geoff Hayward and get on to this press statement?
TED: Sure.
LAURIE: One thing I want to make perfectly clear before I agree to sign anything is that I won't have you coming down to the bench and trying to tell me how to run the game like you did last week.
TED: Danny was getting thrashed. I thought you mightn't have noticed.
LAURIE: What do you think I am? An idiot?
TED: Why didn't you shift him?
LAURIE: Who would I have put on Wilson? The obvious choice would have been pin-up boy Hayward but he was playing like a slug on tranquillisers.
TED: What about Holford?
LAURIE: Holford? Holford was holding our whole back line together. If I had've moved Holford their forwards would have run riot.
TED: Well, I still think you should have done something. And there was no need to bellow at me. I was only saying what everyone else at the ground was thinking.
LAURIE: It's easy to see things wrong from up in the grandstand, but I'm the one who's down there on the spot and I'm the one who knows exactly what my men can and can't do, and I don't appreciate interference from amateurs.

TED: I was only trying to help, Laurie. ~~Your reputation suffered quite a bit of damage over that mistake.~~
LAURIE: ~~It wasn't a mistake.~~
TED: ~~All right.~~ Let's forget the whole business and get onto the press statement. I was—(*hoping that*)
LAURIE: One more thing. Next time the negotiating sub-committee thinks of spending money on a player, I'd like to be consulted.
TED: You will be. We just didn't have time.
LAURIE: Bullshit. You and Jock and Gerry got your eighty thousand and you weren't going to let anyone else in on the act, despite the fact that you were specifically instructed by the full committee to consult me before any purchases were made.
TED: We were scared that the committee might reverse its decision to give us the money so we did things in a hurry.
LAURIE: I'll say you did. You spent the whole eighty thousand on a dud.
TED: You're wrong, Laurie. That boy's a champion.
LAURIE: It doesn't matter how much natural ability he's got. If his heart's not in it he's a dud. Why didn't you go for Fulton Masters and Andy Payne. You could have got both of them for that price.
TED: I did at first. Masters at any rate. I didn't think of Payne. I was going to couple him with Franky Davis.
LAURIE: Davis is a bit past it but even that combination is a hell of a lot better than splashing it all on Hayward.
TED: I think you're wrong. I thought the same way as you do at first, but I suppose it came down to quality versus quantity in the end.
LAURIE: Who stuck out for Hayward?
TED: Jock. We couldn't shift him. He wanted Hayward and that was it.
LAURIE: Jock. Do you want to know something? Jock is an old bastard. Two years ago he was thumping the table in Committee meetings and yelling at the top of his lungs that the Club would never stoop to buying players.

TED: I know. I fought the election against him on the issue.

LAURIE: When it happens he's in there organising it. Why in the hell did you offer him the vice-presidency? All his cronies got beaten and he only scraped back in by two votes.

TED: I intended it as a gesture of reconciliation.

LAURIE: More fool you.

TED: Yeah. More fool me. The very first thing I did after the election was to go out and buy the Club the best administrator in the business, and now, eighteen months later, Jock is in cahoots with *my* administrator and the two of them are running the Club.

LAURIE: He's a great survivor.

TED: I don't know why you spend all your time gunning me down. They're the ones with the real power.

LAURIE: I hear you put up ten thousand of your own money?

TED: Yeah. They pulled a last minute bluff and upped the price to ninety. I didn't mind really. ~~I felt as if I'd contributed in a very concrete and personal way to what I thought was a very important step in the Club's history~~. I still think we've done the right thing. That lad'll do great things for us one day.

LAURIE: I hope you're right.

TED: What're we going to say to the press?

LAURIE: Just that we're prepared to keep working with each other and that I've withdrawn my resignation.

TED: I'd like a bit more than that, Laurie. You called me autocratic in the press this morning. Don't you think that calls for some sort of retraction?

LAURIE: The fact that I've said we can still work together will be more or less a retraction.

TED: No it won't. All that means is that you still think I'm autocratic but you've decided to grit your teeth and sit it out.

LAURIE: That's not too far wide of the mark.

TED: Yes, well I want a bit more. I've got my pride. I want to say that we've had discussions, that several misunderstandings have been ironed out, and that we're sure we can re-establish a fruitful and harmonious working relationship.

LAURIE: Is it true?

TED: No, but it sounds good.

LAURIE: I'll say that we've talked with each other and found that we can still work together. That's all.

TED: We shouldn't be fighting like this, Laurie. It's all so ironic. I've always been one of your greatest admirers. Do you remember the day you played your first game?

LAURIE: Of course.

TED: You'd just turned seventeen three days before. Or was it eighteen?

LAURIE: Seventeen.

TED: There was a real sense of occasion and anticipation right around the ground. We all knew already that you weren't just another recruit. We all knew we were going to see the first game of a great new champion and I don't think anyone was disappointed. Do you remember your first kick?

LAURIE: Not all that well. I know I booted a goal, but there was so much adrenalin pumping through me in the first half, that when I came off the field I could hardly remember a thing.

TED: It was magic, Laurie. It really was. I was only fourteen at the time but I can still see it as clearly as if it was a video replay. You read the play and started sprinting for the goal, picked up a long low pass from Wally Baker, steadied, did a beautiful blind turn around Stan Jackson, and slammed it through the centre. I've seen every game we've played since I was six and I remember that one better than most.

LAURIE: Yes, it was a good game. I settled down in the second half and everyone seemed pretty pleased when I ran off the ground.

TED: Pleased? They went bloody wild. Do you know that right up until the time I was twelve I used to cry every time we lost. If we won I went home and booted a football around our back yard in the dark trying to remember every kick of the match and pretending I was in the side. Hah! By the time I was sixteen I could barely hold my place in the school thirds.

LAURIE: We've all got different talents.

TED: I *would* like to put harmonious somewhere in that press statement, Laurie.

LAURIE: You're a trier, aren't you?

TED: It would make me feel a lot better.

LAURIE: Say we've had a long talk and have resolved our differences. That's as far as I'll go.

(JOCK *comes in the left door*.)

JOCK: I got on to Geoff and he's on his way in.

TED: You're a hard man, Laurie. I'll write it out and give it to Gerry.

LAURIE: I want to check it before it's released.

TED: Don't worry. I won't slip anything in.

(TED *leaves through the right door*.)

JOCK: Geoff's on his way in.

LAURIE: Ted tells me that you were the one who held out for him.

JOCK: Yeah, I did. He is good, Laurie. He's got so much talent he's a bloody freak. He just needs to be motivated properly.

LAURIE: What's this I hear about Parker resigning?

JOCK: Parker resigning? Is he?

LAURIE: Come on, Jock. I'm not an idiot. Gerry said there's some sort of storm blowing up that's going to force him to resign.

JOCK: Yeah, I did hear a whisper to that effect.

LAURIE: Come on, Jock. You don't *hear* whispers, you start 'em. What's going on?

JOCK: He's got himself into some sort of trouble but I don't know the details. Thank Christ is all I can say. I mean let's face it. The man's a buffoon. He's got to go.

LAURIE: And when he goes you'll be standing for President?

JOCK: If it's the wish of the Committee. I'll tell you

something, Laurie. With Parker out of the way things'll start ticking over smoothly again and we'll come out of this trough. You wait and see. Gerry's got some great ideas for next year.

LAURIE: Oh he has?

JOCK: Yeah. A great administrator, that lad. Getting him's one of the smartest things the Club ever did.

LAURIE: You were the one man on the Committee who voted not to appoint him.

JOCK: A man can be wrong.

LAURIE: Not many can manage it as often as you.

JOCK: I'm glad I laid you out behind the lockers.

LAURIE: What are some of these great ideas of Gerry's?

JOCK: We're going to buy up big.

LAURIE: Buy more players?

JOCK: No, sheep. We're going to graze 'em on the oval and save on lawn mowing costs. Of course we're going to buy more players. ~~We're going to go on the biggest buying spree in the history of the game, and what's more it's good economics.~~ Gerry and I have been negotiating —

LAURIE: Why?

JOCK: If we win a premiership it'll arrest the membership decline and members mean money. As a businessman myself I can see the logic of it.

LAURIE: As a businessman yourself. God help us. I was one of the mugs who invested in your import business. A hundred dozen pop-up Taiwanese toasters that burnt the bread then fired it like mortar shells. No wonder the Chinese don't invade them. There's probably a hundred thousand of those toasters permanently trained on the mainland. Then we had the forty gross of Russian alarm clocks that ticked so loudly that the alarm wasn't needed because there was no bloody way you could get to sleep, and the eighty dozen pairs of toy handcuffs from the Philippines that had to be withdrawn from sale after three days because forty-seven kids had to be hacksawed out of them.

JOCK: I'm glad I laid you out behind the lockers.

LAURIE: Well you haven't exactly distinguished yourself in your business career.

JOCK: You won't make fun of me when you hear some of the names we're negotiating with.

LAURIE: (*sharply*) Negotiating? Who's negotiating? Listen Jock, I'm supposed to be consulted—(*when there's*)

JOCK: Not negotiating. I didn't mean negotiating. All we've done is started to think of some names.

LAURIE: Who has?

JOCK: Gerry and I.

LAURIE: What names?

JOCK: Try these for size. Cam Donaldson, Mickey Dimisch and Andy Payne. How'd you like that lot on your goal-to-goal line?

LAURIE: I'd love 'em on my goal-to-goal line but I'd like to be consulted.

JOCK: You are being consulted. Right now. Cam Donaldson, Mickey Dimisch and Andy Payne. Good enough?

LAURIE: Are they available?

JOCK: No, but they will be. ~~Gerry's amazing, but for Christ's sake keep those names under your hat. There's half a dozen clubs after all of 'em. Next year's going to be a good one, Laurie. With you at the helm and players like that in the team there'll be no stopping us.~~

(GERRY *enters through the right door holding a notebook in his hand.*)

GERRY: Is this all you're prepared to say to the press, Laurie?

(LAURIE *reads the statement.*)

LAURIE: Yes.

GERRY: You're not very generous. Ted's pretty upset.

LAURIE: Tough. What's this I hear about Donaldson, Dimisch and Payne?

JOCK: Sorry, Gerry. It just slipped out.

GERRY: (*coldly*) The rate at which things slip out around here makes me wonder if members of this Club aren't fitted with a special circuit that goes straight from ear to tongue and completely bypasses the brain.

LAURIE: What's the meaning of starting to plan next year's team without even consulting me?

GERRY: I was going to talk to you about it today, only you went and got yourself into this mess with Ted.

LAURIE: Where are you getting all the money for this spending spree?

GERRY: We'll get it.

LAURIE: How?

GERRY: Leave that to me.

LAURIE: Be buggered I'll leave it to you. Listen. I've been around here for twenty-seven years and I'm coach of this bloody Club, not the office boy. How are you getting the money?

GERRY: Keep it quiet then. It's all touch and go at the moment. We had two of the biggest property developers in the country in the members bar last Saturday—

LAURIE: Arthur Mowbray and Dick Tanner?

GERRY: Yeah, and despite what Ted thinks they didn't get there by accident. I fossicked around and found out that they're both old supporters so I've been courting them, and doing it pretty well even if I do say so myself. Most guys of that age and in their position are looking for an interesting sideline, pastime, hobby—and these two are no exception, except that they won't have anything to do with us while Ted is President. They haven't said anything directly but it was quite obvious what they were feeling and I can't say I blame them. He was fawning on them like a drunken toad on Saturday.

LAURIE: What sort of role in the Club are you planning for them?

GERRY: If we get rid of Ted we can put Mowbray in as Vice-President and make Tanner an honorary life member.

LAURIE: Where's his twenty-five years active service?

GERRY: We'll get around that. Shit, Laurie, let's not be bush lawyers when there's this sort of money involved.

LAURIE: What sort of money?

GERRY: Two hundred thousand each for starters. If we can't buy ourselves a premiership with that nobody can.
JOCK: We'll collect a bit of cash from our sales as well.
LAURIE: What sales?
GERRY: (*glaring at* JOCK) I was going to discuss the possibility of offloading one or two of our older players who are still looking good but who are just about over the hill.
LAURIE: Such as?
GERRY: I don't know. I'm just an administrator, you're the expert. Given that we get Donaldson, Dimisch and Payne, who could we do without?
LAURIE: Tony Harper, I suppose.
GERRY: Hardly worth the effort. His market price is somewhere under five thousand.
LAURIE: Market price?
GERRY: I've been making a few enquiries.
LAURIE: They're men, not pigs.
GERRY: All right. If you want to mince words we'll call it something else, but the fact remains that there is a market mechanism operating, there is a price on every player and the price on Tony Harper is so low it's not worth negotiating his sale. The only player we've got that has big money on his head is Danny.
LAURIE: We're not selling Danny.
GERRY: Why not? With the players we're getting do we really need him?
LAURIE: (*angry*) Yes of—
GERRY: It's a question. I wouldn't know whether we need him or not. I'm just the administrator and you're the expert. There's no need to get angry. I'm merely posing a question.
LAURIE: We need him.
GERRY: Fine. A few of the wise heads around here seem to think he's looked better than he really is for years because he hasn't exactly been playing in a team full of champions. They're worried that if he plays too many more games like last Saturday a lot of people will start to realise it and his market price, or whatever you like

to call it, will plummet.
LAURIE: Which of the "wise heads" around here believe that little theory?
JOCK: ~~I do~~. I say sell him while he's still worth something. Let's face it, Laurie, when we were winning our medals it was in a team full of champions. Danny's little more than a talented hack.
LAURIE: Come off it, Jock. He's bloody near as good as either of us were in our day. I know what's worrying you. If he stays around for another couple of years he'll beat your two hundred and eighty-two games.
JOCK: Yeah, well you couldn't beat it and he's not going to either. Bloody leaves his wife and kids for an Avis girl. When my record goes it'll be to someone with a bit of moral fibre.
LAURIE: Moral fibre? I don't seem to recall that you were famous for your celibacy in the old days Jock. In fact if my memory serves me—
GERRY: That's enough. Laurie, what if I told you I could swap Danny for Tony Marchesi?

(LAURIE *looks at* GERRY.)

That's made you stop and think, hasn't it?
LAURIE: Can you?
GERRY: No, but it made you stop and think, which goes to show that the central assumption of the science of economics—that we'd all sell our grandmothers if the price is right—isn't all that far wide of the mark.
LAURIE: (*defensive, irritated*) The only reason I'd want Danny to go is if Danny wanted to go. I don't care if you could swap him for Jesus Christ.
JOCK: With the team we'll have next year, Jesus Christ will be pushing to make the reserves.

(*There is a knock at the left door.*)

That's probably Geoff. How do you want to handle this, Laurie? I'll have a chat to him first if you like.
LAURIE: I'll talk to him, if you don't mind.
JOCK: Suit yourself. ~~I just thought that a fresh viewpoint~~

~~might help break the deadlock. I was a coach for fifteen years myself and I have had the odd bit of experience with troublesome recruits.~~

LAURIE: (*tersely*) Clear out and let me talk to him.

JOCK: Suit yourself.

(JOCK *goes to the left door and brings in* GEOFF HAYWARD, *who is medium to tall and looks and moves like an athlete in top condition.*)

Come in, Geoff. ~~Sorry to interrupt your meal. Gerry and I are just going next door to have a drink so that you can have a little chat with Laurie.~~ Feel free to call me if you need me, Laurie. Sometimes a fresh viewpoint can break a deadlock.

LAURIE: Thank you, Jock.

(JOCK *and* GERRY *leave through the right door.*)

You've read the morning papers, I suppose?

GEOFF: Yep.

LAURIE: The Committee are meeting in just over an hour to decide whether they're going to accept my resignation. I think they're going to ask me to reconsider it but it's hardly worth my while if you're going to keep defying me.

GEOFF: So what are we supposed to do? Kiss and make up?

LAURIE: I don't want you to defy me in front of the players again.

GEOFF: I don't want to be told to do push-ups again.

LAURIE: If you break discipline you do push-ups. Everyone does.

GEOFF: I don't.

LAURIE: Nobody else objects to push-ups.

GEOFF: That's because most of them have got ear to ear bone.

LAURIE: I see. You've done a few subjects at University so you're out of our class.

GEOFF: If you like doing push-ups I must be.

LAURIE: All right. Point taken. You don't like push-ups,

but it goes deeper than that, doesn't it? Why are you playing so badly?

GEOFF: I'm doing my best.

LAURIE: No you're not. You played two good games at the start of the year, you went to pieces in your third game and you've got progressively worse ever since.

GEOFF: I've lost form.

LAURIE: It's more than that. You're not even trying. Is it just that you object to me personally or is there some other reason?

GEOFF: I've lost form. That's all.

LAURIE: Look, I know there's some degree of antagonism from the other players. You came to the Club with a big reputation and a lot of money so there's bound to be, but it's not going to help matters if you lay down and stop trying.

GEOFF: You're reading too much into it. I've lost form.

LAURIE: It's more than that. Last week you stood down on the forward line staring into the crowd for over a minute. The ball came and you let it go right past you. Look, level with me, Geoff. That's more than being out of form. What's going on?

GEOFF: All right. If you really want to know, what's going on is that I'm sick to death of football and I couldn't care less if I never played another game in my life. It's all a lot of macho-competitive bullshit. You chase a lump of pigskin around a muddy ground as if your bloody life depended on it and when you get it you kick it to buggery and go chasing it again. Football shits me.

LAURIE: I wish you'd let us know your attitude to the game before we paid ninety thousand dollars for you.

GEOFF: If you think you can buy me like a lump of meat then you'd better think again.

LAURIE: You took our money with your eyes open, Geoff. Don't you think you owe us something?

GEOFF: If you're stupid enough to offer me that sort of money I'll take it, but all you've bought is my presence out on an oval for two hours every Saturday afternoon.

LAURIE: We thought we were buying a lot more than that.
GEOFF: Took your money? It was practically thrown at me. You weren't there at that final sign-up session?

(GEOFF *shakes his head ruefully.*)

It was a joke. There were three of my guys on one side of the table and Gerry, Jock and Ted on the other. Jock was looking at me, and I'm not joking, as if I was a giant pork chop. He was almost salivating. ~~I felt sure that any moment he'd bring out a little hammer and test whether my reflexes are as good as they're cracked up to be.~~ I couldn't believe that those three goons were for real. By the time we'd got ourselves through the pleasantries I was getting pretty crapped off and I decided to make myself a bit difficult, so when they shoved the form in front of me to sign, I read it through four times, put down the pen, shook my head and said I wanted more money. I didn't really expect to get any more—I just wanted to establish myself as something more than a tailor's dummy—but it was marvellous. All hell broke loose. Your guys called my guys cheats, Jock thumped our President on the snout, and Gerry sat there stirring his coffee with a retractable biro. I was just about to burst out laughing when I looked across and there was Ted Parker sitting in the middle of all this pandemonium, his face as white as a sheet, scribbling frantically in his cheque book. "Ten thousand," he yelled. "I'll go an extra ten thousand, but that's my limit." Everyone had a ball.
LAURIE: Are you still living with that girl?
GEOFF: Susy? Yes. Why? Do you think she's a corrupting influence?
LAURIE: She didn't seem very interested in your football career when I met her. LAURIE: You really think
GEOFF: She's not. it's macho-competitive bullshit?
LAURIE: She thinks it's macho-competitive bullshit too?
GEOFF: You can't exactly blame her/me, when it gets to the point where we start coming to blows behind the lockers.

LAURIE: How's your jaw?
GEOFF: Still sore. How's your gut?
LAURIE: Likewise.
GEOFF: Push-ups are one thing but slugging me into submission just isn't on.
LAURIE: I know. I'm sorry. I love football and I love this Club and it's a bit hard for me to understand someone who holds both of them in contempt.
GEOFF: Love the Club? Jock, Ted and Gerry?
LAURIE: The Club's not Jock, Ted and Gerry. It's nearly a hundred years of history.
GEOFF: Yeah. Well I missed the history and copped Jock, Ted and Gerry. Honestly, what's an old fool like Jock doing in a position of power?
LAURIE: He was a great player, and whether he deserved to or not he won four premierships when he was our coach.
GEOFF: Didn't he deserve to win them?
LAURIE: We're not here to talk about Jock.
GEOFF: Was he a bad coach?
LAURIE: Yes.
GEOFF: How come he got those premierships then?
LAURIE: (*irritated*) He got them in his first six years, in the days when the best talent in the country was fighting to get a purple and gold guernsey. By the time I took over all of that had long finished.
GEOFF: Someone told me that you were responsible for getting him the sack.
LAURIE: I thought he was coaching disgracefully and I did some lobbying. I'll admit that to anyone. He dosed himself up with whisky before the '67 Grand Final and halfway through the last quarter he took Benny McPhee out of the centre where he was really firing and put him at full forward, where he was never sighted. It cost us the premiership. Why are you so interested in Jock?
GEOFF: I'm not. It just amuses me to see you guys sticking around in this Club for years, having your little power battles, cutting each others throats and filling up your lives with petty nonsense. So Jock was a bad coach

and you lost a premiership. What does it matter? It's not important.

LAURIE: I might be old fashioned but it seems important to me to step in and do something when a great Club's going downhill because of incompetent coaching.

GEOFF: I don't want to play the devil's advocate but you've done some pretty bad coaching yourself lately.

LAURIE: Such as? ~~Such as not taking Danny off~~ [handwritten: Such as not taking Danny off]

GEOFF: ~~Such as not shifting Danny off Wilson last week.~~ He was getting thrashed. [handwritten: last week.]

LAURIE: I know.

GEOFF: Wilson was leaving him for dead.

LAURIE: (*irritably*) I know.

GEOFF: Then why didn't you shift him?

LAURIE: Because he was desperate to keep trying. He's never been that badly beaten before. I know it was the wrong thing to do but Danny's been the backbone of my team for eight years and I felt I owed him something. Besides, I doubt whether there's anyone in the team who could've done any better.

GEOFF: I could ~~beat Wilson.~~ [handwritten: have.]

LAURIE: You? You were down the other end of the ground staring into the crowd!

GEOFF: ~~I could beat him~~.

LAURIE: (*angrily*) I'm getting pretty bloody fed up with your arrogance, Geoff. You've been paid a fortune and you won't even try; ~~and when I try and talk to you about it you give me a lecture about how petty my life is, and to cap it all off you nonchalantly tell me you could beat Wilson when in the last five weeks you've hardly got a kick~~. I was watching you carefully last week and you couldn't even outrun Butcher Malone.

GEOFF: I was stoned.

LAURIE: Drunk?

GEOFF: Stoned.

LAURIE: Marihuana?

GEOFF: Hash.

LAURIE: Why?

GEOFF: Because it feels fantastic. Five minutes after you

smoke it your head lifts right off your shoulders. I wasn't looking out into the crowd, incidentally, I was watching a seagull. Not just an ordinary seagull. It was the prince of seagulls, dazzling me with blasts of pure white everytime its wings caught the sun. The roar of the crowd paid homage to its grace and beauty. You ought to try some, Laurie. It alters your whole perspective on things.

LAURIE: Are you stoned now?

GEOFF: (*nods*) I had a smoke before I came.

LAURIE: Are you addicted?

GEOFF: You don't get addicted to hash, Laurie. Hey, did you see me fly for the ball in the second quarter? I was so far up over the pack I felt like Achilles chasing the golden orb.

LAURIE: Jesus, Geoff. How am I supposed to deal with this?

GEOFF: Just don't ask me to do push-ups.

(JOCK *pokes his head through the right door. He is smiling affably.*)

JOCK: Sorted things out yet?

GEOFF: Not quite.

JOCK: Would you like me to have a talk to the lad, Laurie? Sometimes a fresh viewpoint can help in these sort of situations.

LAURIE: (*irritated*) No.

JOCK: Just give me a few minutes, Laurie. I've got something I want to say to him.

(LAURIE *gets up, looking at* JOCK *in an irritated way, and leaves through the left door.*)

He's got it in for you, I'm afraid, Geoff. Not to worry. We'll sort it out. You did some nice things last week. Not one of your best games but you did some nice things. Glorious mark you took in the second quarter. You just seemed to go up and up.

GEOFF: I felt like Achilles.

JOCK: Who's he?

GEOFF: A Greek guy who could really jump.

JOCK: (*nods*) Some of our new Australians could be champions if they'd stop playing soccer and assimilate. Why did Butcher Malone take a swing at you when you hit the deck? Did you give him an elbow in the gut?

GEOFF: No, I blew him a kiss.

JOCK: That's good. That's subtle. I was a bit more direct in my day, although I did have a little trick that used to throw 'em out of their stride, come to think of it. You know those times when you're half a yard behind your man and he's going for the ball and there doesn't seem any way you can stop him?

(GEOFF *nods*.)

JOCK: Well, the thing in your favour is that everyone, including the umpire, is looking at the ball, right?

GEOFF: Right.

JOCK: Right. Well as soon as your man leaves the ground, get your thumb and ram it up his arse. Works every time.

GEOFF: Sounds effective.

JOCK: It's a beauty. Wait here while I have a piss.

(*As* JOCK *moves to the door he notices that* GEOFF *has taken out a pouch of tobacco. He stops.*)

JOCK: Roll your own?

GEOFF: Mmm.

JOCK: I used to roll my own.

GEOFF: Would you like me to roll you one?

JOCK: Yeah. Thanks. I'll be back in a minute and we'll have a nice quiet smoke and a little chat.

(GEOFF *nods his head as* JOCK *goes out the door. He fishes in his back pocket and takes out a tin. He looks at the door through which* JOCK *has gone, looks at the tin, nods his head and smiles. Blackout and house lights up.*)

INTERVAL

ACT TWO

> JOCK *re-enters. A minute or two or stage time has elapsed.*
> GEOFF *has rolled two cigarettes. He smokes one and hands the other to* JOCK.

JOCK: (*coughing*) Hope you don't smoke too many of these?

GEOFF: Eh?

JOCK: Makes you short of breath. How many do you have a day?

GEOFF: Three or four.

JOCK: Ah, that's no problem. (*Inhaling*) Quite strong. You get a bit used to having it filtered. Laurie's a bit worried about your form lately. I think you're playing well but Laurie thinks you could do better. I do too. I don't think you're playing as badly as Laurie thinks you are but I think you could do better. What do you think?

GEOFF: I think I could too.

JOCK: Good lad. Puts me in a bit of a spot if you're down on form because I was the bugger that stuck me neck out and said we had to get you. The first time I saw you play I knew you were a freak. One in a million. I still think I'm right. Nothing's worrying you is it?

GEOFF: No.

JOCK: No problems with women?

GEOFF: No.

JOCK: Don't screw too many or you'll get the jack.

(*There is a pause.*)

I get the feeling something is worrying you, Geoff.

GEOFF: You could be right.

JOCK: I've got an instinct about problems. Do you want to talk about it?

GEOFF: I don't know whether I can.

JOCK: It won't get any further than this room if you do. You know that.

GEOFF: Thanks.

JOCK: Have you been able to talk about it to Laurie?

(GEOFF *shakes his head.* JOCK *looks pleased.*)

Yeah. It's hard to talk heart to heart with Laurie. He lacks that little human touch. When I was coach I used to spend hours with my men—joking, chatting, horseing around—but Laurie's a bit stand offish. Not really one of the boys, don't you think? Bit remote.

GEOFF: Well he hasn't told me too many jokes.

JOCK: That's right. No sense of humour. None at all, Bit of a fanatic don't you think?

GEOFF: He lives for football.

JOCK: Right. I used to take the boys up to a country race meeting sometimes in the middle of the week to break the tension and we'd have a few beers and a laugh and it was great. But Laurie would never come. He'd stay back and train by himself in the middle of the oval for hours and hours. ~~Bloody fanatic even then.~~ Do the players *really* like him?

GEOFF: They seem to.

JOCK: I can't understand that. ~~He seems too stand-offish. I was one of the boys when I was coach and they'd do anything for me. Of course you'll hear some stories that my men weren't fit but that's all bullshit. I didn't make a god of fitness and overtrain my men like Laurie; but they were fit, and if you hear any stories that my discipline was lax and that I played favourites, don't believe that either. If someone didn't do what I told 'em I tore strips off them whether they were my drinking mates or not. Laurie started all those stories. He's always had it in for me.~~ From the minute he joined the Club he's made it his business to rewrite the Club's history with him as its biggest shining star. He was obsessed with beating my record of two hundred and eighty two games. Absolutely obsessed. He had a bad groin injury and a dicey hamstring and he was in agony every time he went out onto the field but there was no stopping him.

GEOFF: He didn't beat it though, did he?

[margin note: He was a bloody fanatic even when I was coach.]

JOCK: No, he tripped over little Rabbit Rutherford coming out of a pack and did his cartilages with three games to go, and I can't say I was sorry; in fact to tell you the truth, I laughed me bloody head off. No, I'll make no bones about it. I've got no love for Laurie. Not after the way he took over as coach. I know the style of game had changed and I was making a few mistakes—I was brought up on a different brand of football, not this modern play on, killer instinct, steamroller, win at all costs stuff—and if anyone had have put it to me straight and open that I was getting a bit past it I probably would've agreed and stepped down like a man. But that's not Laurie's style. He went around to the members of the Committee behind my back and told them I was drunk during the '67 Grand Final. I had a cold and I had a few sips of whisky, but I wasn't drunk. He'd had his eye on the job for years. He just waited till I made one little mistake and went in for the kill. He'll keep. He's going to get his. He promised that Committee the world and he hasn't won them one premiership. Not one bloody premiership and I've won four. I don't wonder that you're having trouble with him Geoff and I don't blame you at all because you've got real ability and you can see through him. He can't command the respect of anyone of real ability and he never will. What we need around here is a man of authority who can command, because these days it's fear that wins you premierships, Geoff, I'm afraid. These days the game is so bloody tough that you've got to get your players so scared of making a mistake that they go out there and play the game in a state of fucking terror. Fear's what wins you premierships and Laurie couldn't scare a field mouse.

(*There is a pause.*)

Yes, I can understand why you can't discuss anything with Laurie and I just wanted you to know that I'm on side. What's your problem?

GEOFF: It's a bit difficult to know where to begin. It *is*

to do with women.

JOCK: Usually is. Are you going with anyone in particular?

GEOFF: No.

JOCK: What about that tall sheila I saw you with at the Club ball?

GEOFF: She's just a friend.

JOCK: Jesus, I'll tell you what. I wish I had a few friends like that. I don't mind admitting, Geoff, I was having a bit of a perve. Did she know you could see straight through that thing she was wearing?

GEOFF: I think that was the idea.

JOCK: Marvellous looker, Geoff. Couldn't keep my eyes off her.

GEOFF: She's a beautiful girl.

JOCK: So what's your problem?

GEOFF: It's so bloody embarrassing.

JOCK: Get it off your chest.

GEOFF: You'll keep it absolutely secret, Jock. It'd destroy me if it ever got out.

JOCK: It won't get past this room, lad.

GEOFF: It's not that I'm not attracted to women, Jock. I am. Desperately attracted. But when it gets to the vital . . .

(*pause*.)

JOCK: Can't you get your act together?

(GEOFF *shakes his head morosely*.)

Hell.

GEOFF: For Christ's sake keep that to yourself, Jock.

JOCK: Maybe you're training too hard. I could never get it up on Saturday night after a match. Have you—er—always had—er—this sort of problem?

GEOFF: No. At one stage of my life I had no problem at all.

JOCK: Mind you, you're not the only one. There was an article in the Sunday paper that said that the young men of the nation were being swept by an epidemic of impotence. Woman has become the hunter and man the hunted. Bloody unnatural.

GEOFF: I don't think it's that.

JOCK: Have you seen a doctor?

GEOFF: Yes. There's nothing wrong with me physically. It's up here.

(GEOFF *taps his head*.)

JOCK: Yeah, well I'm a bit suspicious of these psychological explanations. Nothing up there (*tapping his head*) could've stopped my old trooper rising to the occasion. Are you sure you're not training too hard?

GEOFF: It's not that. It's my family.

JOCK: Your family?

GEOFF: They've screwed me up. In more ways than one.

JOCK: Yeah?

GEOFF: You don't mind me telling you this, Jock?

JOCK: No, not at all.

GEOFF: It gets pretty sordid.

JOCK: Fire away.

GEOFF: It won't get past this room?

JOCK: Certainly won't.

GEOFF: Have I ever talked to you about my sister?

JOCK: No. I didn't know you had one.

GEOFF: I don't speak about her very often. She was in a serious car accident the night before her eighteenth birthday. I was only fourteen.

JOCK: Badly hurt?

GEOFF: Very. Both legs were amputated above the knee.

JOCK: Hell.

GEOFF: It would've been tragic for anyone—but for someone as young and beautiful as Gabrielle it was shattering. She wasn't just beautiful either, Jock; she was intelligent, warm, cheerful, popular—she had everything going for her. We tried to keep a stiff lip but I was distraught and so were my parents. Every time I looked at her I had to turn my head away so that she wouldn't see me cry, because the last thing she wanted was pity. I just can't tell you how brave she was, Jock. Don't be sad, she'd say. I'm still alive and I've still got my family. I mean Jesus, is that courage, Jock? Is it?

JOCK: That's courage.

GEOFF: One night I heard her crying in the dark in the next room and it became too much for me to bear—is this all too much for you, Jock?

JOCK: No, no, go on.

GEOFF: You're looking a bit pale.

JOCK: No, no. It's just that the tobacco's stronger than I'm used to. Go on.

GEOFF: So I went and lay beside her and held her in my arms and we cried together. For hours. Every night after that I'd comfort her in the same way and we'd lie together crying in the dark, then one night . . . I'm sorry Jock, I shouldn't inflict this story on anyone. You're looking as white as a sheet.

JOCK: It's the tobacco. Honest.

GEOFF: Are you sure it's not getting too heavy?

JOCK: No. Go on.

GEOFF: Well, without either of us knowing quite how or why, we became lovers.

JOCK: Jesus.

GEOFF: We knew what we were doing was wrong. The surprising thing was that we didn't care. It all seemed so right. Can you understand that, Jock? It was wrong but it was right. Can you understand that?

JOCK: No legs?

GEOFF: It sounds sordid but it wasn't. I loved her, Jock.

JOCK: How long did this go on?

GEOFF: Not long. One night when Dad was away on one of his many business trips the light was suddenly switched on and there was my mother.

JOCK: Hell.

GEOFF: Can you imagine how we felt? Can you imagine how she felt? I can still see her standing there. Still young, and still beautiful in a flowing silk negligee and with a look of utter shock on her face. There was nothing she could say to us and there was nothing we could say to her. She turned off the light and went back to her room and we clung together listening to her sobbing. Finally I couldn't stand it any longer. I picked up my sister and carried her to Mother's room and we all clung together crying like lost souls in the dark. Gradually as the night wore on . . . this is too much for you, isn't it, Jock?

JOCK: No, really.

GEOFF: It gets worse.

JOCK: Go on.

GEOFF: Again, I've no idea quite how and why but my mother and I became lovers too.

JOCK: Hell.

GEOFF: Three nights later my father arrived home early from a conference . . .

JOCK: Hell.

GEOFF: He looked at the three of us and said just one thing. "You've killed me, son." Three days later he shot himself. I've been impotent ever since.

JOCK: No bloody wonder.

GEOFF: It's got so bad that every time I run out onto the ground I feel as if everyone's whispering to each other about me. I just can't concentrate on the game.

(JOCK *frowns and takes another puff of his cigarette. He looks at the photos on the walls, blinks his eyes and looks at them again.*)

JOCK: I'm going to have to lay it on the line I'm afraid, Geoff. It wasn't right to get involved with your sister or your mother and I can't pretend I'm not disgusted, but the Club must not suffer because you happen to have no moral bloody sense. The thing in our favour is that no one knows about it, so thinking that anyone's whispering about you is nonsense and you just better get out there and start playing.

(JOCK *turns, looks at the photos again and frowns.*)

That bloody tobacco's made my eyes go funny. I'll swear I saw those photos move. Quite frankly I had my doubts about paying eighty thousand for a Protestant—if a good Catholic lad so much as even thought of screwing his handicapped sister he'd still be down on his hands and knees yelling Hail Marys—but the damage is done. I held out for you and I'm the one that's going to be crucified if any of this ever comes out. I've got all kinds of enemies around this place and most of 'em are up there on that wall.

(JOCK *looks at a particular photo.*)

Look at that frown on Jimmy McPhee. Look at all of them just itching to sit in judgement.

(JOCK *turns back to* GEOFF.)

This is worrying, Geoff. Extremely worrying. They know that I was the one responsible for getting you. The word gets around.

(JOCK *turns again to the photo of McPhee.*)

Wipe that bloody frown off your face, McPhee.

(GERRY *comes in through the right door as* JOCK, *with his back to him addresses the photo.*)

You shouldn't even be up on the bloody wall. You only played eighty-nine games and none of 'em were worth a cracker. Hacks and dead-beats the lot of you. The only photo that should be up there is mine. Two hundred and eighty two games and four premierships!

GERRY: What in the hell are you carrying on about?
JOCK: We're in trouble, Gerry. Big trouble.
GERRY: We will be if you don't pull yourself together.

(*He takes* JOCK *aside.*)

I've just got a phone call from Bob. The whole thing's hitting the press sooner than we expected.
JOCK: The stuff about Geoff?
GERRY: What stuff about Geoff?
JOCK: He's a nut.

GERRY: If he gets too hard to handle we'll sell him. Now pull yourself together. The stuff about Ted is hitting the press on Sunday. What's that smell?

JOCK: Ted?

GERRY: Yes, Ted. You'll just have to cut down on your drinking, Jock. You'll jeopardise our whole plan of operations. The stuff about Ted is coming out on Sunday. We can probably force him to resign tonight.

JOCK: Sunday? That's earlier than we expected.

GERRY: I just said that.

JOCK: We could probably force him to resign tonight.

GERRY: I just said that too. Now get yourself into shape before the meeting. It's going to be a tough night.

(GERRY *storms back through the right door.* JOCK *turns to* GEOFF.)

JOCK: Yeah, well look, my boy. I'm going to put it to you right on the line. Stay right away from your family and concentrate on the Club. There are really exciting things happening here next year and if you want to miss out on it all, then we'll bloody well sell you.

GEOFF: What things?

JOCK: We're getting some great new players and a fantastic coach. Oh shit. I shouldn't've said that . . . What *is* wrong with my head? Just keep that quiet. Laurie's had his chance and last week was the last straw. He's done his dough. A five year old could've seen that Danny had to be taken off Wilson.

GEOFF: Who's the new coach?

JOCK: The best. The very best. We're throwing out the old tradition that the coach has to have played for the Club.

(*He turns to the photos.*)

Why should these old hacks get first go at a plum job? We're going for the very best. We're getting great players too, so if you pull your socks up and start trying you could find yourself the star in a team full of champions; so stop feeling sorry for yourself and start trying or we'll cut our losses and sell you to a deadbeat team up the Mallee.

(*There is a knock at the door and* LAURIE *enters from the left.*)

LAURIE: Are you finished, Jock? I'd like another word with Geoff.

JOCK: Yeah, I'm finished. You remember what I said, Geoff. I'm not joking.

(JOCK *leaves through the right hand door.*)

LAURIE: What was all that about?

GEOFF: Jock got a little bit heavy.

LAURIE: Well, I'm going to get a bit heavy too. I'm not very impressed with your attitude, Geoff. Danny's down below playing pool. He hasn't got half of your natural ability or your brains; he's fucked up his personal life and he's coming to the end of his football career, but he's thrown every ounce of his energy for the last ten years into doing as well as he possibly could for the Club and for me; and I admire that, because if you've got talent you've got a responsibility to use it and not fuck around. So if you're ever out on that field again and you're not a hundred per cent fit, a hundred per cent clear headed and a hundred per cent trying then you'll never play another game for this Club in your life, Selection Committee or no Selection Committee. You look me in the eyes, Geoff, and listen to what I'm saying. You might think it's a big joke to smoke and screw and take Ted down for ten thousand dollars; but I don't think it's all that funny.

GEOFF: I didn't take him down.

LAURIE: You took him down.

GEOFF: He took himself down, the stupid little turd.

LAURIE: All right, he's a stupid little turd. He's also seen every game this Club's played since he was six years old and I know that that's the last thing that'd impress you, but by Christ it impresses me.

GEOFF: What's ten thousand dollars to him? He's rich.

LAURIE: He's not. He's about to go bankrupt. Now maybe I'm just feeling guilty about what I did to him in the press this morning, but I promise you if you don't start playing football then I'm going to make you give him back every cent of his money, even if I have to pound it out of you. Right? Look at me?

GEOFF: Laurie, you're giving me the shits.

LAURIE: And so are you. If you're really on about love and peace and non-competitiveness then pay back your money and get out. Get out for good and don't fuck around. If you hate the game and all it stands for, then get out; but I'll tell you one thing—you'll miss it. I've seen you swelled up with bloody pride out there. I've seen you so bloody pleased with yourself that you've had tears in your eyes.

GEOFF: Bullshit.

LAURIE: It's not bullshit. Don't think I couldn't tell what was going on in your mind when you took the opposition apart in the first match. You thought that you were fantastic. You thought that you were the greatest footballer alive.

GEOFF: It was good. So what. So is being stoned and making love to Susy.

LAURIE: Anyone can get stoned and make love to Susy.

GEOFF: That's a pretty distasteful assertion.

LAURIE: You know what I mean. It's a great feeling when you're out there playing well and you're going to miss it. I ought to know. I've been missing it for fifteen years. If you want my honest opinion, the reason you're into drugs and non-competitiveness is that you tried a few things that didn't come off in your third game and you've been scared ever since.

GEOFF: Scared?

LAURIE: Yes. Scared that you're not half as good a footballer as you bloody well thought you were. You're in the top league now, Geoff, and there's lots of competition. It's no good saying you *could* beat Wilson, you've got to *do* it.

GEOFF: Don't try that one on me.

LAURIE: You're scared.

GEOFF: Lay off the primitive psychology, Laurie.

LAURIE: We've got Taylor against us tomorrow. It's no good telling me you *could* beat him either. You've got to *do* it.

GEOFF: I've watched these sort of films too, Laurie. What I'm supposed to do now is leap up and say: "I will. I'll eat the bastard for breakfast," and go out and play the game of my life. Is that right?

LAURIE: If you're not scared, then why do you have to drug yourself up before you go out on the field?

GEOFF: Because football bores me. I've done it all, Laurie. When I was twelve I was living in a little country town and my ultimate dream was to get a game in the local firsts. Six years later I was picked in the State side. I was an acknowledged champion.

LAURIE: No you weren't. You were just a young kid with a lot of potential and you still are. Anyone who wasn't cross-eyed and bandy-legged could get a game with the Tasmanian State side. When you've got the guts to go out there and take on proven champions like Wilson and Taylor, and when you start to miss the roar of the grandstand, then come back and tell me you're trying. Until then you can sit and rot in the reserves for the arrogant young turd you are.

GEOFF: I'm more than a kid with potential, Laurie. Tasmania's provided this State with more champions than you can name. They don't pay eighty thousand dollars for a kid with potential.

LAURIE: Normal people wouldn't, but as you've pointed out, this Club is run by morons. Now if you don't come to your senses I'm going to drop you to the reserves for the rest of the year, and the year after that and the year after that. As far as I'm concerned you can play out the rest of your career in the reserves and be damned to the eighty thousand dollars. Now get out of here and don't come back until you mean business.

(GEOFF, *who is angry at* LAURIE'S *dismissal of him as a 'kid with potential', opens his mouth to reply, but sees that*

LAURIE *is in a towering rage, so he shuts it and leaves through the left door.* LAURIE *takes out a packet of cigarettes and lights one, trying to calm himself.* TED *enters through the right door looking agitated and angry.*

Have you sent out the press statement?
TED: They're trying to force me to resign.

(TED *moves across to the presidential chair at the head of the committee table.*)

LAURIE: What do you mean, force you?
(GERRY *enters through the right door followed by* JOCK.)

GERRY: I just thought you might *want* to resign. That's all.
TED: There's no way in the world I'm going to resign.
GERRY: It's up to you, Ted. I'm sure the Committee will back you if you want to battle this whole thing through.
TED: I'll battle it through and I'll expect a hundred per cent loyalty from the Committee.
JOCK: You won't get it from me.
TED: I wouldn't expect it from you. Or from Laurie. But I'll get it from the rest.
JOCK: If you were a man you'd step down right now.
TED: Cowards duck. Men fight.
JOCK: Fight who? Women?
TED: You believe her story, I suppose. Every word.
JOCK: Why shouldn't I? Gerry was there.
TED: I slapped her. That's all Gerry saw.
GERRY: You hit her at least once, Ted.
TED: I slapped her.
GERRY: If it comes to the point of testifying, I'll say that I was confused and I wasn't sure what you did. But you did hit her.
JOCK: With closed fists too, you mongrel. Don't expect me to be sorry for you.
LAURIE: What's going on?
GERRY: Ted's in trouble, Laurie. A stripper's suing him for assault and the whole thing's going to be

plastered over the Sunday papers.
LAURIE: The stripper at the fund raising night?
TED: I didn't hit her. It's a load of trumped up garbage. If the Committee sticks with me, we'll see it through.
LAURIE: I thought you only fumbled with her garter?
GERRY: He followed her around backstage.
TED: She egged me on all through her act, Laurie. Eyed me off, stroked my hair, asked me to take off her garter —played the vamp for all she was worth, but then when I went around backstage she switched it all off and treated me as if I was dirt under her feet. Nobody treats me like that, Laurie, least of all a little trollop like that. I'm the President of the greatest football Club in the history of the game and I won't have some little slut laugh in my face.
LAURIE: (*to* GERRY) Was she hurt?
TED: Of course she wasn't. I hardly touched her, but by the time the journalists have got through with me it'll sound like we went fifteen rounds.
LAURIE: How did the press find out?
GERRY: God knows. We've been doing everything possible to keep it quiet at this end.
TED: The Committee's got to support me. If everyone's behind me we can fight it through.
JOCK: I'm not supporting you, you mongrel. The medical report said she had bruises all over.
TED: What medical report?
GERRY: (*hastily*) Oh the . . . er . . . newspaper rang me to see if they could get a Club reaction to the incident and they mentioned a medical report that's in the hands of the girl's lawyer.
TED: I slapped her, Gerry. You've got to testify that I only slapped her.
GERRY: I'll say that I was confused. I can't say that I definitely didn't see you hit her if they've got a medical report that mentions extensive bruising. I'd go up for perjury.
TED: She must have got one of her friends to slap her around so that she'd get more money out of me. It

happens all the time. I gave her twenty dollars and she was quite ready to forget the whole thing. That's how upset she was. She's gone away and thought about it and decided to make some easy money out of me.

GERRY: I wouldn't be surprised if you're right, but the public are going to believe her rather than you.

TED: (*with a touch of hysteria*) Who gives a stuff what the public believes? The facts are that she called me a pig and I slapped her. I'm the greatest President this Club has ever had. I've singlehandedly wrenched it out of the stone age against pressures that would've broken a lesser man. I've fought a pitched battle against the forces of tradition and conservatism and I've won; in fact I've been so bloody successful that those very forces have turned around and adopted my ideas as if they were their own.

JOCK: Are you referring to me?

TED: (*with more than a touch of hysteria*) Yes, I am referring to you. I've changed the whole future course of this Club and because of what I've done the next years are going to be the greatest years we've ever had. We're going to have a triumph that'll make the great years of the '20s look pale by comparison. We're going to dominate the League for the next decade and I'm going to be here while we're doing it. No little trollop is going to deprive me of that! The Committee will stick by me to a man.

JOCK: You want to bet.

TED: I'd stake my life on it.

JOCK: Then you're a dead man. The Club's not going to let its name be dragged through the mud just to save your hide, Parker. I'm going to move that you stand down.

TED: You won't get a seconder.

JOCK: Want to bet?

TED: Even if you do you won't get the numbers on committee.

JOCK: Want to bet?

TED: Who have you got?

JOCK: Tony, Ian, Jack and Kevin for starters.

TED: Bullshit. They don't even know about it yet.
GERRY: They do. I rang around as soon as the paper rang me.
TED: Ian and Kevin are my friends, Jock. If anyone's going to stick with me they will.
JOCK: Want to bet?
GERRY: The one thing you've got to understand, Ted, is that if the consensus is that you do resign, then it's not necessarily because we don't think you're innocent or that we're not your friends, it's just that because we're on the Committee we've got to face realities, and the reality is that it isn't so much whether you're innocent or not that counts—it's whether the public think you're innocent; and in this case, I'm afraid, the public are going to think the worst. We just can't afford to jeopardise the credibility of the Club by retaining a President who's erred in the way that they're going to think that you've erred.
TED: What kind of logic is that?
GERRY: It's the logic of pragmatism, Ted. You ought to know that. You brought it to this Club and you were right. Loyalty to any one individual is a luxury you can't afford in a business with a multi-million dollar turn-over. I'm sorry, Ted. I don't particularly like the brutal side of pragmatism either and I'll vote to retain you; but if the majority of the Committee ask for your resignation I hope you can understand their viewpoint.
LAURIE: They're going to get you, Ted. Get out gracefully.
TED: Laurie, I've had my differences with you but I've been a good President. Not a great one but a good one. They're not going to sack me if I lay my record on the line.
LAURIE: They don't need you any longer, Ted. If they didn't need me they'd sack me too.

(TED *looks at* LAURIE *knowing that* LAURIE *is in fact to be sacked. He realises that his dismissal is inevitable and gathers the remnants of his dignity together.*)

TED: Nobody's going to sack me, Laurie. I've just resigned.
GERRY: I'm sorry that this has happened, Ted. You've been a good President and you won't be forgotten. You fought to get me my job here and I won't forget that either. I just hope I can go on to do justice to the faith you showed in me.
TED: (*blackly*) I'm sure you will. (*To* LAURIE) I hope that you and young Geoff sort out your differences. I'd like to think that my money was well spent, I doubt if I'll ever be dashing off ten thousand dollar cheques again.
LAURIE: I don't think your money will have been wasted.

(TED *puts on his overcoat and moves towards the left door.*)

TED: (*To* LAURIE) Do you know what I thought was the best game of football you ever played? The day you took on Dick Turner in '55. Mind you, I think he just shaded you. By a whisker.
LAURIE: A lot of people don't.
TED: It was like watching two magicians trying to outdo each other.
LAURIE: I think everybody got their two bob's worth.
TED: (*to* GERRY *and* JOCK) I'm not running away. I could stay here and fight and probably get the numbers but I couldn't be bothered. I've got a bedridden wife to look after and I've run out of energy and I don't even know whether it's worth fighting when the Club's fallen into the hands of people like you. You've been scheming to get rid of me for six months and the gods have delivered me into your hands, but one day when the true history of the Club is written I'll have pride of place over you two vultures. I'll be amongst the very great ones.

(*He leaves.*)

GERRY: Poor bastard. I feel sorry for him.
JOCK: Sick in the bloody head.

GERRY: He did hit the girl. ~~I had a hunch that something might happen when I saw him head off so I followed him~~. It was a hell of an ugly scene. The girl was quite hysterical.
JOCK: Mongrel. What kind of man hits a woman?
GERRY: He was screaming out that he was the President of a great club and belting her with closed fists. I put a headlock on him and dragged him off.
LAURIE: Why didn't she call the police?
GERRY: I calmed her down and gave her twenty dollars, but the poor kid was only eighteen and had never stripped before and a couple of days later she freaked out and just about went off her head.
LAURIE: What day was that?
GERRY: Last Monday.
LAURIE: Who was the girl you and Jock were talking to on Tuesday?
GERRY: What girl?
LAURIE: In your office. I came to see you and your secretary said you were busy and a couple of minutes later a young girl came out. Jock was in your office too.
GERRY: We must have been interviewing someone for a secretary's job.
LAURIE: Come on. She was no secretary. Was she the stripper?
GERRY: No. Her flatmate.
LAURIE: Why was she there?
GERRY: What is this, Laurie? A Star Chamber?
LAURIE: Why was she there?
GERRY: She came to tell us that the girl who'd stripped was on the verge of a breakdown. She was having bad nightmares and wouldn't move outside her flat.
LAURIE: Did she ask you for more money?
GERRY: Yes.
LAURIE: So what did you do?
JOCK: We told her that if she wanted money she'd better go to Ted. It was nothing to do with the Club.
LAURIE: Ted hasn't got any money.
JOCK: That's not our bloody fault. She wanted the Club

to pay a thousand dollars and we weren't going to come at that.

LAURIE: So what'd she do? Go to the papers?

JOCK: We didn't tell her to go to the papers. All we said is that if her flatmate was in a bad way then she should go to a lawyer.

LAURIE: And sue Ted?

GERRY: He's still got property and if the little kid is in a bad way she deserves every penny she can get.

LAURIE: You'd spend eighty thousand dollars for one player but you wouldn't spend a thousand to keep the Club President off the cover of a scandal sheet.

GERRY: If the kid's in a bad way she deserves every penny she can get.

LAURIE: I'm sure she does, but if it hadn't've suited you to get rid of Ted right at that minute you would've written that cheque for a thousand dollars without a second thought. You put the press onto it too, didn't you?

JOCK: So what. He deserves every thing he gets, the bloody little upstart. Comes in here and takes over the Presidency and he's never played a game of football in his life.

LAURIE: I won't hold you up. You probably want to go in there and drink to your success.

GERRY: I can't see why you're getting so bloody moral about all this, Laurie. You carted him into the press yourself this morning.

JOCK: Yeah, he's not exactly your favourite person. I'd pay a thousand dollars to get him *in* a scandal sheet. What a bloody disgrace to the Club. Hitting a woman. What a bloody disgrace to those champions up there.

(JOCK *indicates the photos on the wall.*)

LAURIE: Do you know what, Jock?

JOCK: What?

LAURIE: You're a hypocritical old bastard.

JOCK: Well it is a bloody disgrace.

LAURIE: I would've thought that a man who's given his

wife as many black eyes as you have wouldn't be quite so self righteous.

JOCK: You're too smart for your own good Laurie. You've needled me and picked at me from the very first minute you came here.

LAURIE: Underneath that rough charm of yours that's served you so well over the years, Jock old mate, there's a cunning and ruthless old turd.

JOCK: You've had it in for me ever since I laid you out behind the lockers.

LAURIE: That certainly didn't help. A tap on the shoulder and a king hit before I could raise a finger in my defence, but I shouldn't've been surprised. I knew what you were all about long before that. I saw the last game of football you ever played.

JOCK: Bullshit. You would've still been in nappies.

LAURIE: I was six, and I'd wormed my way right down to the fence. What was the name of that little guy you flattened?

JOCK: You weren't there.

LAURIE: Yes I was. In fact the whole thing happened only about twenty yards away from where I was standing. You waited until he started to pick himself up off the ground, lined him up, and went straight into him with your knee. He was about five foot seven and ten stone. What was his name again, Jock?

GERRY: That's enough, Laurie.

JOCK: He wasn't as badly hurt as the papers made out.

LAURIE: He did recover. Eventually. Some people think that you retired after that match out of remorse but I know you better. The Club was told by every other club around the League that if you ever took the field again you'd be lucky to get off it alive.

JOCK: They didn't scare me.

LAURIE: Not much they didn't.

JOCK: Nobody's ever called me a coward before.

LAURIE: Well I'm calling you one now, and if you're going to be our new President then it's my last year as coach.

JOCK: It's going to be your last year in any case, smart-arse. We're going to get ourselves a real coach here next year, thank Christ, so stick that in your pipe and smoke it.

(JOCK *storms out through the right door.* GERRY, *furious that this information has been disclosed, glares at* JOCK *as he passes.*)

LAURIE: Am I being sacked?

GERRY: There's some talk that your contract mightn't be renewed. Some of the Committee feel that you've had a fair chance and haven't come up with the goods.

LAURIE: Who are you getting?

GERRY: I don't think anyone's got as far as thinking about that.

LAURIE: (*indicating photos*) There's no one up there who's as good as I am.

GERRY: I think there's some talk of dispensing with the tradition that the coach must have played for the Club.

LAURIE: I see. Just like that. Well, there's no need to ask who you're after.

GERRY: He gets results.

LAURIE: Yes, he does.

GERRY: You've had eight years, Laurie, and you haven't come up with the goods.

LAURIE: I haven't had the players to come up with the goods, and the reason that I haven't had them is that all through those years Jock kept thumping the table, pointing to those photos and shouting that the Club had never paid for its champions in the past and it wasn't going to start now. All right. He won four premierships. With the players he had I could've won ten. You can't do this to me, Gerry. I've worked my guts out for eight years bringing ratshit teams up off the bottom of the ladder. If you give me half of the names that have been mentioned here tonight I'll win you a premiership.

GERRY: I don't doubt it. The irony of this whole situation—and I know that this isn't going to make you feel any better, is that I've done a thorough check around the traps and after Rostoff you're considered the next best coach in the business. Different styles of course, but no one doubts your effectiveness. The chances are that you could win us that flag, but the Club's been waiting nineteen years and the Committee wants to be absolutely sure. We've got a two million dollar annual turn-over and you can't afford to risk that sort of money on sentiment. Do you see our point of view?

LAURIE: Yes. Quite clearly.

GERRY: You'll have no trouble finding another team to coach.

LAURIE: I don't want another team to coach.

GERRY: Try not to get too angry, Laurie.

(LAURIE, *in a fury, stares at* GERRY. JOCK *bursts in through the right door.*)

JOCK: I've been called all sorts of things in my time by sports writers, Laurie, but never a coward!

LAURIE: That says more for the severity of our libel laws than it does for your courage.

JOCK: What about you? Sneaking around behind my back and telling the Committee I was a drunk so you could get my job. Do you call that courage?

LAURIE: You'd just lost us a premiership.

JOCK: I notice that you didn't win us too many when you took over.

LAURIE: And you know why I didn't.

JOCK: Oh, I'm to blame for that too, am I?

LAURIE: You and your cronies wouldn't let me buy players.

JOCK: We were upholding an old tradition. We were wrong, but we believed in it.

LAURIE: They might have believed in it but the reason why you wouldn't let the Club buy players was to stop me winning a flag.

JOCK: That's crazy talk, Laurie. Do you honestly think I'd sabotage the Club for eight years just to get back at you?

LAURIE: Yes, I do.

JOCK: Well you're crazy. It's just as well we're getting rid of you.
LAURIE: You were a thug as a footballer and a failure as a coach. You're the last person who should be our President.
JOCK: You can call me what you like, Laurie, but the record books are going to show that I played three more games than you did, and won four more premierships, and they're still going to be saying it in a hundred years.

(JOCK *leaves through the right door.*)

LAURIE: I'm going to fight this, Gerry. I'm going to go to every member of the Committee and tell them what an oily little weasel you are.
GERRY: It won't do you any good. They've made up their minds. Their first loyalty is to the thousands of supporters out there who want a premiership: and so it should be. If the Club doesn't think like that, then it won't survive.
LAURIE: If this Club survives by spreading a man over the front pages of a scandal sheet and sacking a man who's never been given a fair chance to prove himself, then its survival isn't of much importance.

(LAURIE *goes to the wall and takes down his own photograph.*)

I love this Club and I love the game, Gerry, and my photo's not going back up there until you and Jock are gone.
GERRY: I don't love the Club and I don't particularly like the game and that might make me an oily weasel in your eyes, but I'm the best football administrator in the country and you're only the second best coach, so don't count on being able to return that photo for quite a long while.
LAURIE: Get out of here, Gerry, or I'll bloody well take you apart.

(GERRY *leaves through the right door.* LAURIE, *with his*

photo tucked under his arm, picks up his coat and turns to leave.
GEOFF *enters.*)

What do you want?

GEOFF: I'm looking for Ted.

LAURIE: He's gone.

GEOFF: I've written a cheque for him. For ten thousand dollars.

LAURIE: Good for you.

GEOFF: You won't be able to hold that over me again.

LAURIE: I'm not interested in holding anything over you. I just want to know if you're going to start trying, because if you're not, you're going straight down into the reserves. I meant what I said.

GEOFF: I'll do what I've been paid to do. Is that your photo?

LAURIE: Yes.

GEOFF: Have they told you you're getting the sack?

LAURIE: Yes. How did you know about it?

GEOFF: I heard it from Jock.

LAURIE: It seems that everyone's heard about it except me. Look, Geoff. I'm asking you for the first and last time for your help. You're not just a kid with potential, you're an amazingly bloody talented footballer, and I want you to take over the centre from Danny tomorrow.

GEOFF: Danny's not going to like that.

LAURIE: Let me worry about that. You're the only one in the team that can match Taylor so I want you to play centre. I want to win that game very badly and give the Committee a kick in the teeth.

GEOFF: I don't like our chances.

LAURIE: Neither do I if you're going to be a pessimist right from the word go. We can win.

GEOFF: It'd be a hell of an upset if we did.

LAURIE: You did lose confidence after that third game, didn't you?

GEOFF: A little bit.

LAURIE: There's no need to be touchy. It happens to all of us. I only got seven kicks in my third game and for the next four matches I wasn't worth a cracker. Stand away from Taylor at the first bounce and I'll get Alan to knock it to you instead of Keith. If you get that first kick and do something with it you'll be right for the rest of the match. I'm sorry I asked you to do fifty push-ups but if you're playing under Rostoff next year you'll have three assistants noting down every mistake you make and at half time you'll be screamed at and told you're a gutless turd in front of the whole team.

GEOFF: (*gloomily*) I thought they might be getting Rostoff.

LAURIE: Yeah, well they haven't got him yet. If you play well enough and the team plays well enough for the rest of the year they'll find it pretty hard to sack me.

GEOFF: Do you think?

LAURIE: If we make the finals it'll be pretty embarrassing for them.

GEOFF: Finals?

LAURIE: It's not impossible.

GEOFF: I suppose not.

LAURIE: If we win twelve of the next fifteen games we'd make it.

GEOFF: It doesn't sound so impossible when you put it like that.

LAURIE: It's not impossible.

(DANNY *knocks and enters through the left door.*)

DANNY: Still going. Don't waste your time on him.

LAURIE: It's O.K. Geoff's going to start trying.

DANNY: About time.

LAURIE: They're sacking me, Danny.

DANNY: When?

LAURIE: At the end of the year.

GEOFF: They're getting Rostoff.

DANNY: Rostoff? Like hell they are. I'll call the boys.

LAURIE: No strikes, Danny. If you really want to help me the best thing you could all do is to try like hell for the rest of the year.

DANNY: Try like hell?

GEOFF: They'd find it pretty hard to sack Laurie if we made the finals.

DANNY: Bastards. We'll win the bloody flag.

LAURIE: We won't win the flag but we could make the finals.

DANNY: It'd help if moneybags here got off his arse and started trying. Put him on Taylor tomorrow.

LAURIE: Taylor? (*To* GEOFF) I suppose that if you did go well on him, you'd get your confidence back.

DANNY: Put him on Taylor. Make him earn his money.

LAURIE: I'll think about it.

DANNY: Are you taking your photo?

LAURIE: I don't want it hanging up here.

DANNY: Good idea. Let's take the rest. They wouldn't want to be up here either. (*To* GEOFF.) Give us a hand.

(DANNY *and* GEOFF *start taking down the photos.* LAURIE *watches them. They use chairs to reach the photos high on the walls.* GEOFF *pauses and looks at a particular photo.*)

GEOFF: Did Harry Payne really kick three goals in time on in the '23 Grand Final?

LAURIE: Yeah. Dad was playing on the forward flank and set one of them up for him.

GEOFF: Is your dad's photo up here?

LAURIE: No. He played most of his football in the reserves.

DANNY: He could have been a regular in any other club.

LAURIE: He probably could've but he didn't want to shift. Keep that ten thousand, Geoff. If you start playing well, Ted'll think his money well spent.

(GEOFF *looks at* LAURIE, *obviously a little puzzled by the remark, as he is not aware of its full implications.* DANNY *meanwhile, has stopped in front of* JOCK's *photo. He looks at it, takes it off the wall and calmly drops it to the ground.*)

DANNY: I dropped Jock.

(GEOFF *looks at* DANNY, *who is standing on a chair*

looking down at JOCK's *photograph.*)

GEOFF: Don't let it lie there. Jump on it.

(DANNY *descends from the chair and resumes taking down photos.*)

DANNY: We shouldn't be too cruel to Jock. He's always been very good to his mother.

GEOFF: I can imagine.

DANNY: No. Really. On the twenty-ninth of May, no matter where he was or what he was doing, he'd always send her a bunch of flowers and a telegram of congratulation.

GEOFF: Was the twenty-ninth her birthday?

DANNY: No, his.

(GEOFF *and* LAURIE *laugh.* LAURIE *picks up his jacket and turns to go. But before he can leave,* JOCK *and* GERRY, *having obviously heard the noise of the breaking glass, enter through the right door.*)

GERRY: What's going on?
DANNY: I dropped Jock.
GERRY: Where are you taking those photos?
DANNY: We haven't decided.
GERRY: Is this some kind of juvenile protest?
DANNY: Yeah. If the Committee notices that they're gone, they might ask themselves why before they go appointing Rostoff.
JOCK: What're you doing helping this lot, Geoff?
GEOFF: I don't want Rostoff, either.

(GEOFF *and* DANNY, *who have been working away at a fast rate through the preceding dialogue, now have all of the photos off the walls.* LAURIE *opens the door for them as they each carry a stack out.*)

GERRY: I hope this gives you some small satisfaction, Laurie?
LAURIE: Yes, it does.
GERRY: All of them will demand that their photos go

straight back up ~~there as soon as Rostoff wins them a flag. Probably earlier.~~ when you're gone and we start winning.
LAURIE: Possibly.
GERRY: You've got young Geoff back on side, I see?
LAURIE: Yes. Geoff's going to play very well for the rest of the year. We're going to win quite a few games.
GERRY: Don't think that it'll make any difference to your position, Laurie. I thought I'd made that clear. ~~The Committee are certain Rostoff will win them a flag and they're not certain that you will, and in the end that's the only argument that's going to count.~~
LAURIE: Possibly, but I'm going to put the counter argument to the Committee that a premiership that's won the way Rostoff wins them isn't one that they'll be particularly proud of.
GERRY: Do you really think they'll listen?
LAURIE: They might. Despite what your economics books tell you I'm not convinced that pragmatism is absolutely irreversible.
JOCK: Don't get all excited about getting Geoff onside, Laurie. He's totally bloody erratic. He'll be cutting your throat again tomorrow.
LAURIE: No he won't.
JOCK: Yeah, well I know something about him that you don't.
LAURIE: Good for you. See you at the game tomorrow.

(LAURIE *leaves*. GERRY *turns on* JOCK *in fury*.)

GERRY: You've been a great help tonight. ~~You told them about Rostoff and~~ now they're all prepared to fight, and you go and get Geoff in here and now he's all reconciled with Laurie. What'll happen if the Club starts winning for the rest of the season?
JOCK: It won't matter. ~~Everyone on the Committee wants Rostoff now.~~
GERRY: I wouldn't trust the Committee as far as I could kick them. I can get rid of a moralistic coach any day, but a moralistic coach who's winning games could be bloody hard.

JOCK: They want Rostoff.
GERRY: What's this stuff you know about Geoff?
JOCK: He's bloody unstable. First thing we do next year is sell him.
GERRY: Sell him?
JOCK: Yeah. He's been up his mum and his legless sister and he thinks he killed his old man.
GERRY: (*staring*) What?
JOCK: He confided in me, so don't tell anyone—although—hey! If he starts playing too well we can always leak a rumour or two.
GERRY: Jock. Geoff has two brothers, no sisters and his father had his fifty-fourth birthday last Saturday. Now get inside and try and sober up before the meeting.

(GERRY *storms off in a rage, followed by a frowning* JOCK *carrying his broken portrait. They leave a denuded Committee room behind them.*)

END

THE PLAY IN THE THEATRE
Rodney Fisher

Having now directed the premier performance of David Williamson's last three plays—*The Department*, *A Handful of Friends* and *The Club*, I feel confident in saying that Williamson has two great talents, over and above his singular ear for dialogue and his sharp instinct for dramatic structure. They are firstly his adherence to that old adage, much quoted, not always observed: "Write about what you know." Secondly, that since there is little exotica or eccentricity in Williamson's background as a country bank officer's son studying engineering, his adept selection and juxtaposition of what he knows is such that what at first may seem banal or trivial can suddenly be profound.

Williamson is, in fact, a playwright enjoying total rapport with his audience. So readily do Wiliamson's words strike gold at the box office and so spontaneous is the audience response that it is easy to underestimate his craft, to suspect some trick or sleight of hand. It has sometimes been the case for Williamson to be isolated, even dismissed, as some sort of nine-day wonder whose knack for serving up what the audience wants is bloody amazing, but whose writing is of only passing worth. It is my experience that Williamson enlarges and illuminates his audience's perception of itself and explores intricate sub-texts where it has been assumed that no such sub-texts exist.

It is as well to remember too that Williamson plays in subsidised theatres to the genuine general public. He is the only Australian playwright to repeatedly do this. With a few notable exceptions, most new Australian plays are courageously endured by regular theatre subscribers in the hope of a double helping to follow of sequin-studded Shakespeare or, heaven help us, Sheridan. Williamson enjoys a continuing success story with all major subsidised theatre companies and brings his own following with him. In the case of the Melbourne Theatre Company, which has presented the majority of his plays, the subscribers have made it clear that Williamson is not their particular brand of Twinings' tea and stay away, while the non-theatregoers of Melbourne pack the usually off-limits Russell Street Theatre to capacity each evening at eight-fifteen for every Williamson performance.

Williamson's ability to connect with his audience—and let me add that his audience is remarkably diverse in age, education and social status—is largely due to his respect for it. He does not pander to it, patronise it or necessarily agree with it; but he respects it. In the same way, he respects the people he creates on stage. He does not caricature them or unnecessarily embellish them. He respects them. This is basically what the magic of Williamson's name on the billboard is all about: Williamson's modest expectation is that the audience will know what he is talking about and the audience's expectation is that Williamson will generously reward them with the pain and laughter of self-recognition and a greater awareness of the world they live in. They are rarely disappointed. In my own case, Williamson has significantly altered my perception of my fellow Australians. I am sure I am not the only one.

It is no mean feat. We are a complex and self-conscious lot in Australia. Our traditional sense of inferiority manifests itself under various guises that range from diffidence to boozy aggression but seldom include soul-searching confrontation or the flash of self-criticism. So Williamson has fossicked out of his experience those areas of life where circumstance or obsession allows a group of people to behave in a manner untypical of themselves—moments when they feel liberated to express themselves undercover, as it were, from real life.

In early plays—*Don's Party* and *Jugglers Three* in particular—excessive alcohol was the circumstance or catalyst. Most recently, the obsessional worlds of the department head estranged from his wife, who gives his life to his job and the ambitious film director who yearns to equate commercial success with creative prowess, have provided circumstances for the sort of public unbuttoning which is both characteristically Australian and quint-essentially Williamson.

In *The Club*, which I would class as Williamson's most technically assured piece of work to date, he takes on the fanatical world of sport and concentrates on those who are obsessed by it. In Melbourne, Australian Rules Football has as fixed a place in the hearts and minds of the population as the Melbourne Cup or complaining about the weather. It is a public pastime which consumes thousands of newspaper column inches each year and to which radio and television devote most of the weekend and a good part of the rest of the week as well.

Any institution so monolithic has detractors as well as admirers and Aussie Rules is always ripe for caricature, albeit difficult as anyone who sampled the television series *And The Big Men Fly* will know.

But Williamson is not a caricaturist. He has disturbed a subculture in which the world of private lives and wives has taken a back seat to a preoccupation long since grown to obsessional proportions. In *The Club*, Jock, Ted and Laurie are locked in mortal combat; Gerry manipulates them; Danny and Geoff are incensed by the process but must live with it. Thus, it is not only a truthful tale about football but a dissertation on politics and a microcosm of the world outside. Moreover, because football is "only a game" — and "tradition" and "honour", "record books" and a "multi-million dollar turnover" are involved — the characters are freed from the laconic, diffident, mainly silent image reserved for their family and wives; and throw themselves, boots and all, into self-revelation and aggressive confrontation.

Pre-publicity for *The Club* when it was about to premiere in Melbourne inevitably emphasized the "90,000 dollar recruit". Consequently, the delayed appearance onstage of Geoff Hayward tended to whet the audience's appetite — conditioned no doubt by *And The Big Men Fly* — for a joke: a naive, hulking yobbo or something of the sort. Williamson, however, spares us any such excess. He gives instead a finely wrought combination of arrogance, uncertainty and appeal, a character who ultimately must make a decision which wins for him the respect of the audience. It is a decision which David Williamson has long since made for himself: that however much you may disagree with a system, however proficient you are at exposing or deflating it, you must — whatever the cost to your pride — join it before you can begin to change it.

Brisbane, 1977